About The Reader

The Reader magazine is published by **The Reader**, a not-for-profit organisation within the University of Liverpool. The organisation has grown out of the magazine, which was launched when the founder editors were literature teachers in the Continuing Education programme. In what seemed a unique community, free from the constraints of exams or accreditation, readers aged 18–80 and from all educational backgrounds were sharing reading difficulties and enthusiasms. There was a sense of exhilaration: we were reading big and daunting works together with growing confidence. The desire to keep that spirit alive is behind everything we do.

The Reader magazine first appeared in 1997. We continue to provide a platform for personal and passionate responses to books, as well as seeking to identify new and exciting writers. We also publish a free newsletter which details our events and projects.

Events include **Readers' Days**, where people from all walks of life come together to discuss books, stories and poems; large-scale public events like the **Penny Readings**, which look to recreate the meetings where Dickens would read to thousands; and live events featuring authors as diverse as David Constantine, Doris Lessing and Will Self. **The Reader** also offers tailored training for organisations that wish to put reading into the heart of their work.

The Reader's participation programme, **Get into Reading**, is our largest area of work, actively seeking out new readers in non-traditional or disadvantaged areas. We believe that literature has a purpose in the world beyond the syllabus, classroom or lecture hall, and that its absence from common life is a loss to be remedied. We set up weekly reading groups where facilitators read aloud, ensuring that the words are made real for readers and non-readers alike. This makes a **Get Into Reading** group profoundly democratic and leaves the power – to join in and to speak, or to remain silent and private – entirely with the individual. Group members report increased confidence, concentration and motivation.

The Reader

No. 23, Autumn 2006

Editor	Jane Davis
Co-editors	Sarah Coley
	Angela Macmillan
	Brian Nellist
	John Scrivener
	Helen Tookey
Student assistants	Kerry Hughes
	Gareth Finn
	Alan Maloney
	Jonathan Mercer
	Eileen Pollard
New York editor	Enid Stubin
Contributing editor	Les Murray
Address	The Reader
	19 Abercromby Square
	Liverpool L69 7ZG
Email	readers@liverpool.ac.uk
Website	www.thereader.co.uk
Subscriptions	see p. 123
Cover picture	by Emma Gregory

ISBN 0-9551168-2-1
   978-0-9551168-2-7

Distribution information   p. 128

Submissions

The Reader welcomes submissions of poetry, fiction, essays, readings and thought. We publish professional writers and absolute beginners with emphasis on quality and originality of voice. Send your manuscript to: The Reader Office, 19 Abercromby Sq., Liverpool L69 7ZG, UK. **New York Office,** Enid Stubin, 200 East 24th St., Apt. 504, New York, NY, 10010. SAE with all manuscripts please.

Published by The University of Liverpool School of English.
Supported by:

Printed and bound in the European Union
by Bell and Bain Ltd, Glasgow

contents

readers connect

reviews

recommendations

the back end

" Look out in this issue for quotations from John Keats and
George Eliot's *Middlemarch*. **"**

The Written Troubles of the Brain

Jane Davis

Macbeth: How does your patient, doctor?
Doctor: Not so sick, my lord,
         As she is troubled with thick-coming fancies,
         That keep her from her rest.
Macbeth: Cure her of that:
         Canst thou not minister to a mind diseas'd,
         Pluck from the memory a rooted sorrow,
         Raze out the written troubles of the brain,
         And with some sweet oblivious antidote
         Cleanse the stuff'd bosom of that perilous stuff
         Which weighs upon the heart?
Doctor: Therein the patient
         Must minister to himself.
                              (*Macbeth* V iii)

We are not all Macbeths but something of that couple's striving, guilty situation is our own. Lady Macbeth is not so much ill as 'troubled' by the thing which Macbeth, suffering too, calls 'that perilous stuff / Which weighs upon the heart'. As their doctor says, in such a case no one can help: the patient must minister to himself. That word 'minister' is interesting. The verb can't escape the noun: minister, a priest, spiritual carer. As a verb 'to minister' is primarily a caring word and almost always carries a health implication. Macbeth's doctor, understandably, is certain that *he* can do nothing to help: the patient, troubled by what we'd now call OCD, washing imaginary blood from her hands, must look after her own (spiritual) welfare. It is too late for Cognitive Behavioural Therapy.

Neither can the doctor help the husband. There's a wonderful controlled Shakespearean pronoun slippage from Macbeth saying 'Cure her of that' to the doctor's 'minister to himself'. We start with the wife but are very quickly talking about the husband. But even before the doctor says 'himself', while Macbeth is still speaking, we know it is himself Macbeth is talking about. The solipsism of his disease means he can't keep hold of the imagination of another's plight for long. The degeneration of his humanity is so complete that all a doctor can sensibly do is make a run for it. Or call for a priest.

Reading the magazines and weekend supplements, watching those almost pornographic TV ads for the finest mozzarella and balsamic vinaigrette salad, one could be forgiven for thinking that life – here, now – is a bed of roses. As indeed, for many of us, it is. We are richer and healthier than our grandparents could have imagined, we have access to life-saving, and life-prolonging, medical treatments, we are better housed and fed, we live longer, own more labour-saving devices, and enjoy an astonishing range of things to buy or dream about. But even so, though the outer world doesn't always let on, it remains true that, as Thoreau said in *Walden*, 'the mass of men live lives of quiet desperation'.

You long for a baby and miscarry. Or you cannot get pregnant and spend eight years in unsuccessful IVF treatment. Or you successfully conceive and give birth to a child who develops a mysterious and life-threatening illness. Or she is run over on her way home from school aged 12.

You cannot find the right partner and drift from one unsatisfying relationship to another until you decide to give up on love and become the spinster aunt. Or you do find the right partner and he develops testicular cancer and you spend the first three years of your marriage in that battle. Or your partner is a drinker, a gambler, is unfaithful, is not what you thought.

You have no job. You hate your job. You are bored by your job. You lose your job.

Your old dog gets older, loses his mobility, is dying.

You and your husband live well into old age and one by one your generation, all the people you have known, friends who married at the same time as you, relatives you've warred with for years, begin to die.

Human culture has for thousands of years prepared people to cope with the fact that 'man is born to trouble as the sparks fly upward' but since we've been well-off we seem to have forgotten that resource. Post-natal depression is on the increase, a health visitor tells me, because 'people are surprised that having a baby doesn't solve all their problems'. 'Most of my depressed patients aren't depressed,' says one inner-city GP to me. 'They just need something to do.'

We don't address the nature or the source of these problems, preferring to buy our way out of trouble. We are more likely to run to the doctor than to call for a priest and the doctor, hard-pressed for time, is likely to prescribe a pill. In the UK we are spending over

£400 million a year on antidepressants (see www.mind.org.uk). For some, these prescriptions are lifesavers, but for many, as most GPs acknowledge, the SSRI drugs are causing more problems than they are curing.

A new idea in creative health circles is the 'books on prescription' scheme – where sets of self-help books are available for doctors to prescribe. Good idea but wrong emphasis. Despite their huge sales, self-help books don't work for everyone: you need to be the kind of person who can already minister to yourself, follow a programme, *stick to something*. They are like diet books: you buy them instead of doing it. For most of us, if we could follow the common-sense advice such books offer we wouldn't need a book in the first place. We're more stuck and much less rational than that.

When, not so long ago, the Bible was about the only book available, and its stories were shared by all, sorrow was part of the main agenda. These days only daytime TV shows take it on: 'my wife came back to life', 'my babies were murdered by a psychopath', 'my sisters killed my father' – to take some themes from Shakespeare. Yet Shakespeare is the stuff of exam syllabi, not of general adult reading (which seems to comprise *Celebrity Lovelife / Fat Spotter* magazine). By relegating anguish, sorrow, regret, and all the other feelings of pain and disappointment 'that flesh is heir to' to some out of sight out of mind place, we are creating a huge unaddressed backlog of 'that perilous stuff / Which weighs upon the heart'.

In the past, doctors, like priests, often provided support for the sick and their families; their vocation, while dealing with the absolute materiality of our sickening bodies, also in some sense involved something beyond the material. When we are unaccountably unhappy what we need is not a pill or anti-depression manual but something much simpler, more effective, and more rare. We want compassion (com + passion = suffering with); we want the human companionship which in a less medicalised age was the very stuff of good doctoring. In *Wives and Daughters* (1866), Mrs Gaskell gives us Dr Gibson, a country doctor, as scientific as a provincial man could be in 1840, whose humanity is an absolute given for his daughter Molly, much to the discomfiture of his new second wife, who must learn what it means to be married to a doctor:

> 'I feel so lonely, darling, in this strange house: do come and be with me, and help me to unpack. I think your dear papa might have put off his visit to Mr Craven Smith for just his one evening.'
> 'Mr Craven Smith couldn't put off his dying,' said Molly, bluntly.

'You droll girl!' said Mrs Gibson, with a faint laugh. 'But if this Mr Smith is dying, as you say, what's the use of your father's going to him in such a hurry? Does he expect any legacy, or anything of that kind?'
Molly bit her lips to prevent herself saying something disagreeable. She only answered, –
'I don't quite know that he is dying. The man said so; and papa can sometimes do something to make the last struggle easier. At any rate it's always a comfort to the family to have him.'
'What a dreary knowledge of death you have learned for a girl of your age! Really, if I had heard all these details of your father's profession, I doubt if I could have brought myself to have him!'
'He doesn't make the illness or the death; he does his best against them. I call it a very fine thing to think of what he does or tries to do. And you will think so, too, when you see how he is watched, and how people welcome him!'

Dr Gibson may do something to lessen physical suffering but it is the non-material comfort of his presence, the suffering alongside, the compassion that is, as the daughter divines, truly helpful. Nowadays GPs spend on average 8–10 minutes per consultation. We cannot afford the time compassion might take. But why must we always look to our overstretched GPs for this?

I should like to see a Reader-in-Residence at every Health Centre, to bring poems to the waiting room, to read stories aloud, to engage the disengaged in conversation, to bring the lost and lonely together in weekly reading groups. These groups might help buoy up patients suffering a wide range of ills. Poetry on prescription, discussed and meditated on alongside others, might offer a form of compassion and leave our GPs free for medically treatable disorders. Fanciful? Yes, but only in the imagination of such a national scheme. The efficacy of the cure has been pointed to for quite a while.

In chapter 5 of his autobiography the philosopher and social thinker John Stuart Mill gives a detailed personal account of depression cured by poetry:

It was in the autumn of 1826. I was in a dull state of nerves, such as everybody is occasionally liable to; unsusceptible to enjoyment or pleasurable excitement; one of those moods when what is pleasure at other times, becomes insipid or indifferent… In this frame of mind it occurred to me to put the question directly to myself:

'Suppose that all your objects in life were realized; that all the changes in institutions and opinions which you are looking forward to, could be completely effected at this very instant: would this be a great joy and happiness to you?' And an irrepressible self-consciousness distinctly answered, 'No!' At this my heart sank within me: the whole foundation on which my life was constructed fell down. All my happiness was to have been found in the continual pursuit of this end. The end had ceased to charm, and how could there ever again be any interest in the means? I seemed to have nothing left to live for.

...I became persuaded, that my love of mankind, and of excellence for its own sake, had worn itself out. I sought no comfort by speaking to others of what I felt. If I had loved any one sufficiently to make confiding my griefs a necessity, I should not have been in the condition I was...

What made Wordsworth's poems a medicine for my state of mind, was that they expressed, not mere outward beauty, but states of feeling, and of thought coloured by feeling, under the excitement of beauty. They seemed to be the very culture of the feelings, which I was in quest of.

It seems to me fascinating that John Stuart Mill is able so precisely to locate the power of Wordsworth's poetry ('medicine for my state of mind') in its provision of a model for, and a language of, 'the feelings, which I was in quest of'. For Mill, these particular poems, at this particular time, gave ground where feelings could come back into being: 'the very culture of the feelings'. This is what is most lacking in contemporary public and perhaps private life. We are not educated to recognise or understand our feelings, or to trust or use them. Literature in general, and certain kinds of poetry in particular, offer a language for feelings – the written troubles of the brain – and what a waste it is for us not to prescribe ourselves a trip to the bookcase or library, book group, bookshop, internet poetry site as a first port of call when we need help. That literature has a *practical* use seems so odd that is almost unsayable. We don't have any trouble with understanding the notion of reading as escapism – perhaps that is what Macbeth calls a 'sweet oblivious antidote'. But to read in order to do yourself some good? Liberal sensibilities will be afeared of that: someone will have to make value judgements about what constitutes 'good'. But therein the patient must minister to herself. And let's be pragmatic. If such a scheme helped 1 person in 1000, think how it could cut that £400,000,000 pharmaceutical bill.

Editor's Picks

Susan Fox's wonderful poem, 'Conspiracy of One', tells the story of old Mr. Iskowitz, who seems confused but who may actually be the brightest and most cogent of us all. The city of New York is glimpsed in all its life and scale around him on his journey to the May Day Parade. (p. 27)

Raymond Tallis, 'Read from the Top', demonstrates powerfully why literary people are richer for lending attention to the scientists who explore beyond our usual boundaries. At once humane and microscopically accurate, the story offers a stunning collision of two spheres: life as *matter* side by side with life as it is *experienced*. (p. 24)

Readers Connect. We launch our new feature for reading in groups. The idea comes directly out of our experience of how good discussion works to command and to deepen attention. We figured that by the time you've read three rollicking articles on each featured novel, you'll be hooked. It works. At least one of our editors has been drawn eagerly to the programme and claims to be 'the first customer'. (p. 75)

Ask the Reader: an unsung part of *The Reader* and at the same time the best *The Reader* has to offer: 'We need more Shakespeare and Tennyson and less Valium and I look forward to the day when the GP will prescribe *King Lear* or bits of *Don Juan* or *The Waste Land* as sovereign remedies for our ills'. (p. 118)

O thou whose face hath felt the Winter's wind,
   Whose eye has seen the snow-clouds hung in mist,
   And the black elm tops 'mong the freezing stars,
To thee the spring will be a harvest time.

John Keats, 'O thou whose face hath felt the Winter's wind'

The Reader/Blackwell Poetry Competition

To mark the publication of John Redmond's How to Write a Poem, *Blackwell Publishing and* The Reader *magazine recently staged a poetry competition, judged by the poet John Redmond,* The Reader *editor Jane Davis, and the poet Patrick McGuinness. In the following pages, and in a richly combative style, Redmond and McGuinness consider the state of poetry today. Happily, the judges were (largely) of one mind in the end, and* The Reader *is proud to present the runners-up and special commendations, and especially the competition winner, Laura Webb.*

Winner

Laura Webb
Lonely Planet

His name was Lee. You knew his face.
The lettering was frail and spaced,
like beads on a cheap necklace, each pearl

a ball-bearing, and holding itself in place.
Somewhere, in a kitchen, he is singing, making breakfast.
Years later, you buy his first-hand

edition of Belgium: Bruges, Brussels and Ghent.
You follow him, turn at his folded corners,
walk the streets he underlined in red,

though nothing is the same. Only his name. See,
the time he's taken over each letter.
Somewhere, a while ago, he is shaking,

gravitating towards the end of his tether.

Runner-Up

Stephen Wilson
Needlework

Just months in the weaving
now here's the wrap, the cover,
tangled as the purled shawl
in which her newborn sister lies.

The silver-tongued thread,
the gentle hold and drop stitch,
cross-stitch, unintended bang-
the-feeding-baby stitch,

the sibling stitch up, the love
crush, the light-as-a-feather
needlepoint, the gros point,
the pinched up smocking,

saintly smile – that life so short,
the craft so quick to learn.

Runner-Up

Adrian Blackledge
Clouds Hill

T.E.L. i.v.35

How surprised they would have been the snooping pressmen
to see us stretched on a silk counterpane
in the reading room as first light changed
from grey to yellow through a crack in the curtains.
Perched in trees binoculars fixed on bedrooms
they have chased me out three times in as many weeks.
Once again I have made a bolt for it
holing up in Westminster with a new name.

But the deadness of demob and pottery
has given way to something entirely new.
I am astonished by the arch of your back
the upward push of your breasts, your fingertips.
Tonight I'll take the old Brough and ride back to you.
It still goes like unholy smoke when I turn the taps on.

Highly Commended

Mark Leech
Becoming Light

To be this fall of light that made it through
bare webbed branches and dusty windows
to stretch like pleasure at your feet, you must
break your nature. Start with long division,
then recombine the fresh numbers until
in every whole you see coexisting
fractions. It's best to do this near a stream,
and next to dive straight in, muddy yourself
as deep as the cold will take you, ripple
with the surface breeze. Let the current tear,
hang stagnant on the ebb, and after this
you'll be ready to start becoming light,
to be both wave and ray, radiation,
particle. By this time the light has moved,
angling for dust down the wall, and now comes
the hardest part: climb inside the minute –
because time and light are indivisible –
remembering to leave your dull body
to one side with your senses and the pile
of things that make you human, a lover
of light. This is what you wanted. To last
from stars to earth, forever beautiful,
forever a fresh beam of purest day.

Highly Commended

Wendy Cook
Barrow

Spread-eagle shag above BAE,
Vickers once, Maxims,
talking premier league here
once...
Moss smears the pink townhall.
Scuttering like rats, McDonald's wrappers blow,
and young and old with not much to do, not much to spend,
                              nowhere to go,
steer shipping-lane ways through tumbleweed streets
where brick-mash sniggers round a sign,
'Building A Brighter Future'.

The town's as baggy as a newkid's blazer.

From out past Walney and the Irish Sea,
the Atlantic air, sensing an opening,
rises like the sea through turf channels.
High-sided tenements funnel the ozone.
People can be the crabs,
and cars the darting shrimps.
But the rock pool is stale.
With each failing tide a few more fail.
The blown heaps of keratin grow.

Past Morrisons a minesweeper anchors in the dock.
Pressed white shirts of her tidy crew carry purpose to a purposeless
                                                            town.
Join the navy, lads.
Why not?
What has not already been lost?
Returned to sea, retired engineers ignite,
though it's now too late and there's no need to know.

A tattooed dad warns shaven-headed kids,
'Keep yer hands in yer pockets or else'.

'Or else wot, Dad?'
'See that guard with his gun…'
And he shows them, as they'll never need to know,
where the front of Seelandia lifted for the train to run
that'll never run no more.

Anything to lose?
Anyone?
Ragbone. Ragbone.

Minesweeper anchors to sweep up the souls.
Live ordnance.
Send a town with workers,
pull out the pin,
the work and the meaning that kept them all in.

Highly Commended

Pauline Suett-Barbieri
The Shirley Valentine Syndrome

What is this thing about stones
that every other poet feels the need
to take one in their clammy hands
and try to tell us how it feels.

A grey pebble won't tell its secrets
to anyone, least of all someone
who's going to tell.
And what surprises me even more

is that it's nearly always a pebble
they go on about. Never a bit of rubble
which could be very revealing.
It's had a lot more work experience.

I saw a man once with an old brick on tv.
He used to talk to this brick in such a way
I wanted to build a house from them.
The problem was the brick wouldn't tell

him where it had come from
and of course it had no DNA.
But it was such a polite kind of brick
he let it lay indoors, on the table.

When friends came they noticed it
but didn't say anything.
Until the brick spoke.
I've never heard a poet talking

about a brick like this which could
be wonderful. I can just imagine
them comparing its colour with
a sunset over the Colorado valley,

its texture with the crumbling painted desert
and its conversation with the purling
of the stream over a pebble
on a hot canyon of a day.

Evasive Work

John Redmond

Since the competition was designed to accompany the publication of my book, *How to Write a Poem*, I think I should reflect on the purposes of the book and how these related to the poems which were actually entered. One of the major aims of the textbook was negative, an attempt to point readers away from the 'default contemporary poem' (one might think of such a default poem as the sum of all the received notions about poetry currently in circulation). *How to Write a Poem* was strongly influenced by the American pragmatist tradition which, like the Irish verbal culture in which I was formed, puts a high value on evasion. The book tries to provoke readers into evading automatic ways of making poems.

But, as many of the entries to the competition demonstrated, automatic assumptions about what a poem 'should' be and what a poet should do are very persistent – it is not easy to go around them. Surprisingly many things are still regarded as 'poetic' in themselves – words such as 'shimmer', 'gleam' and 'linger', places such as shoreline, heath, and forest, archaisms such as 'ye', 'thee' and 'o'er', and material such as gold, silver and diamonds. Writers still use inverted word-orders for no other reason than that it is something which one does when writing verse. And writers are still inclined to confuse the strength of the feeling behind a poem with the strength of the poem.

Whether good or bad, poetry in the UK is fairly conservative and the range of entries reflected this too. Certain styles and periods retain their popularity long after the life has gone out of them. There were poems written in quasi-nineteenth-century style (Wordsworth and Tennyson as models), in Georgian style (the First World War remains a persistent topic), in the style of traditional hymns, and among the more modern models, writers such as Larkin and Heaney were evident influences.

For many people, writing a poem is like dressing up in black-tie. The point of the exercise is to mark out a statement or an observation as 'special', to elevate and dignify an otherwise unremarkable moment. By way of example, ITV recently led their World Cup coverage with a long and rather dull poem in rhyming couplets.

This was not because they wanted to engage in verbal invention but because they wanted to signal that the event they were covering – the World Cup – was exceptional, and therefore, as with a limo at a wedding, a poem was called for.

Linked to this, many contemporary poems seem to be exercises in self-validation. To adapt Neil Kinnock, they are ways of declaring 'I am all right'. The writers of such poems tend to over-identify themselves with their work and so are usually over-sensitive to criticism. Perhaps out of a misplaced sense of politeness, a lot of bad poetry is tolerated in this country. One of the reasons why poetry in Ireland outperforms poetry in Britain is that, in Ireland, it is impossible to open your mouth without receiving criticism. This can be unpleasant, of course, but it also forces writers and talkers to be resourceful, to 'up their game'. Really good poems *never* emerge from uncritical environments and one of the problems with the grant-led British poetry scene of the last few decades has been that it has been interested in the health of people writing poetry rather than with the health of their poems – it has sought to make people feel better about themselves through writing poems, rather than giving their audience better poems to read.

How to Write a Poem emerges at a time when Creative Writing courses are gaining a major foothold in this country. In my view these courses are a good thing because, when well-run, they force writers, early in their careers, into contact with a peer audience. They largely bypass the self-celebrating function of poetry. Happily, the better entries to the competition revealed writers who were weighing the effect of their words on an audience, and who were writing, not just for themselves, but with a range of possible readers in mind. Of these, the best were written with energy, wit and skill, and satisfied repeated reading. I hope that their writers will go on to find wider audiences.

I think poetry should surprise by a fine excess, and not by singularity; It should strike the reader as a wording of his own highest thoughts, and appear almost as a remembrance.

John Keats, letter to John Taylor, 27th February 1818

The Double Bind

Patrick McGuinness

Judging the Blackwell Poetry Competition was an instructive experience. I've entered plenty of poetry competitions in my time (and never won) but this was my first experience of judging one. In one sense, I judge poems all of the time since I teach French literature and lecture to students who want to learn about the subject if not necessarily to practise it. But there's more at stake in what we call 'creative' writing, and correspondingly more at stake when one evaluates it. When I give a poor mark to a student's essay on Baudelaire, I'm making a frank comment on a piece of work. They take pride in that work (I hope), but it's something separate from them. It is filed away and put aside. It's not an expression of themselves, as a poem surely would be. I don't envy the delicate task of the creative writing tutor who, faced with an indifferent poem by a student, has to negotiate the tricky border between helpful criticism and dispassionate judgment.

I have limited experience of this, and it's not especially good: about three months ago a student I didn't know emailed me an unsolicited bunch of poems. He wanted my 'frank opinion'. I read them, thought about them, and wrote back saying that though his poems were full of energy, they were obviously written by someone who didn't actually read much poetry. Perhaps he should read more, I suggested, and gave him a short list of modern poems I thought a new writer could learn from. I was rather pleased with my mix (as I saw it) of tact, encouragement and practical advice. His reply suggested he saw things differently: 'Thank you very much for your comments which obviously I disagree with and are just your personal opinion'.

His poems were not bad but they were written by someone who clearly wasn't sure what a poem was supposed to *do*. Most of the poems in this competition were like that (the winners and shortlisted poets aside, of course, and an armful of unplaced poems too). For a while, as I toiled through the pile of submissions, I couldn't quite make out what was wrong. Was it a question of form? No, I had the same feeling with the sonnets as I had with the free verse poems. Was it a question of subject? Hardly; my reservations extended to poems on a range of subjects, from the mating habits of giant squid to scenes of childhood abuse; and besides, anyone who thinks one subject is more 'poetic' than another probably shouldn't be involved with poetry. Was it language perhaps? No, there were plenty of *thee*s and *thou*s and *yes* and *ahoy*s, and conversely, in other poems, a lot of pseudo-slang that would have worked as pop lyrics (if there were guitar riffs strong enough to muffle them): but those poems weren't any good because, well, they just weren't any good. It was a different category of poem that was both vexing and intriguing me: those that had something good about them but which were somehow wrong, that were written by intelligent, interesting people with something to say, but that just didn't work.

It was when I tried to puzzle out what poets the competitors had been reading that it all came clear: they *weren't* reading. Most of these poets didn't read poetry. I don't mean they didn't live and breathe the stuff, or study it academically, but that they genuinely didn't seem to have read any at all. They just picked up a pen (some indeed sent ornate calligraphic handwritten poems) or sat at their computer and wrote. But wrote what? From where? Of the more than 500 entries there was a good handful of poems with real originality and vigour: they had energy and application, they could turn good images and come up with a memorable line. But even some of these seemed to have been written without any sort of poetic experience. Had the poets ever sat down with a poem they enjoyed and asked themselves *how* it worked, and *why* it worked so well? This isn't a question of mastering forms or applying a method. It's even less a question of 'studying' poetry. It's a question of working out how you want to write, what you'd like one of your poems to do, and why you think a poem can do it and not, say, a letter or a lecture, a diary entry or a good rant in the pub. I don't think you can do that without reading other people.

Someone with whom I discussed this observed: 'Would you enter a singing competition without having trained your voice, a music competition without knowing how to read music, or try for a watercolour contest without a sense of how to paint?' A novel, even a bad novel, requires discipline, organisation, focus. A writer may start lightly, but very soon they realise that a special assemblage of skills on top of the originating enthusiasm is necessary. The novel needs planning, research, time set aside, sustained application, and, especially, reading other novels. These are persuasive analogies, but they're misleading because it *is* possible to write an excellent poem untutored, and without having read much. It just doesn't happen often, and we tend to forget how the first thing an original poet learns is how to mask his or her debts. The raw, untutored, and seemingly spontaneous poem is as much a deliberate construction as the fine-tuned courtly sonnet is. Dylan Thomas's notebooks reveal so many corrections and rewritings that they outnumber the pages of poems by something like five to one. Rimbaud, who propelled the myth of the poet as visionary genius, schooled himself methodically on his elders before telling them they were losers who should step aside. But with poetry, today, it seems, anyone can have a go.

It's ironic that the art which is habitually criticised for elitism, irrelevance, remoteness is the only art pretty much *anyone* thinks they can practice, the only literary form people feel entitled to dabble in with no preparation, learning or training. This is poetry's double bind: it's the victim on the one hand of outrageous amateurishness and on the other of a kind of hermetic, cultish, exclusiveness. The bad faith that surrounds poetry today is to do with the way in which these two essentially negative positions – pseudo-democratic boosterism and snobby mystique – dominate any discussion we try to have. But these two positions are, despite their apparent antagonism, mutually stabilising, and rely on each other for their continued existence. We need to get beyond them by talking about writing poetry as an art that grows from reading poems, and the only real basis for this discussion is that both the reading and the writing should be done well.

It should not be controversial to say that poets should, by and large, read more poems. It has to be permissible to say that there are bad poems, and that these are more likely (by and large – we're not talking absolutes here) to come from people who don't read poems than from those who do. More significant however is the fact that – judging from this competition – many poems that might have been good are being prevented from becoming so because they're written without any sense of where, poetically, they're coming from.

I've chosen not to talk about the excellent handful of winning and commended poems, and working on the basis that one should pick one's battles, I haven't looked for ways of improving the titanic majority of bad poems. I've chosen to address myself to that inter-mediary zone where the contestant definitely had something but could not bring that something to fruition. I find myself back with my unknown student. When I was asked by *The Reader* to write this piece, it was suggested that I complement it with a list of ten poems by modern poets who should be read. I have mostly chosen poets who are slightly off the beaten track but write in ways that are entirely their own. This is not a list of favourite poems, but a list of poems which I think yield good practical and imaginative examples to writers sufficiently interested to think about them, and sufficiently ambitious to aim beyond merely imitating them.

Jorie Graham, 'The Geese'
Thom Gunn, 'Sunlight'
Paul Muldoon, 'Why Brownlee Left'
Donald Davie, 'In the Stopping Train'
Robert Creeley, 'For Love'
Elizabeth Bishop, 'The Man-Moth'
John Ashbery, 'Self-Portrait in a Convex Mirror'
Janet Lewis, 'Fossil, 1975'
Margaret Avison, 'Micro-Metro'
Samuel Menashe, 'White hair does not weigh'

Anniversary Issue of *The Reader*

March 2007 marks a huge achievement for *The Reader* – ten years of publishing essays and poetry and fiction. It has been a worthwhile pursuit, and we are proud to know that we have drawn together a recognisable community of open-minded 'readers for serious pleasure'. So, please, celebrate with us! Readers are invited to write in with favourite articles and memories of the last ten years of the magazine, as well as to share their hopes for what we might go on to do. (Deadline for material 1st November 2006)

The Reader, 19 Abercromby Square, Liverpool, L69 7ZG, UK

Want a year off to write your novel?

A new £18,000 Writer's Bursary has been established, which will allow an aspiring writer to devote a year to writing a novel. The Bursary is open to novice and experienced writers, and candidates are invited to write on any subject, as long as it is substantially a work of imagination and fiction.

The Bursary is open to anyone over the age of 18 years, resident in the UK or Republic of Ireland. The closing date for entries is November 30, 2006. For more details visit www.medicalcasenotes.co.uk/bursary/ or call the bursary administrator on 01843 232 859

The Bursary is being provided by MCNA (Medical Case Notes Assessment Ltd), a medico-legal company based in Margate, Kent.

Read from the Top

Raymond Tallis

This is Dr Rahman's first Monday General Eye Clinic after an absence of six weeks and he is testing the visual acuity of his first patient.

It was Sister who told me that he had had a lobectomy to remove a lung tumour. He had, she said, been coughing up blood for over four months before he had sought help. How she knew this, I don't know. Anyway, within three days of presentation to a local chest physician, he had been admitted to hospital, transfused with blood, and bronchoscoped. Two days after the bronchoscopy had revealed a tumour, he had had his lobectomy. Now, six weeks later, he is back at work in the clinic, in his capacity as Medical Assistant to Mr Rees, the Consultant Ophthalmologist.

No-one had expected him back so soon, as he was entitled to at least another month or two of sick leave. Probably, he had been fed up at home and could see no point staying there, alone, brooding over his ill health and what the future held. Sister told me that he was a widower. His wife had died in India many years ago, giving stillbirth to their first and only child, before she had been able to join him in the UK. He had chosen to be back at work: back to glaucomas and retinopathies, errors of refraction, and orthoptic problems; back to squinting children whose anxious parents do not always conceal the fact that they would have preferred the opinion of Mr. Rees, working only a few feet away; back to old ladies whose worlds are darkened by cataracts, who talk at great length and who cannot understand the questions he asks even when he does raise his voice; back to industrial injuries whose problems are hedged about with the threat or promise of compensation… Back to all that…

We greet him with a slightly awkward warmth. 'If we'd known you were coming, we'd have put out the red carpet', Mr Rees said.

Dr Rahman takes off his jacket, unveiling the old-fashioned braces supporting his baggy trousers, and hangs it on the hook vacated by the white coat he had picked up, just as he had done over the last five years. This would be the last of a series of 'temporary' jobs that have left him, in his late fifties, numbered amongst many doctors who have remained juniors of a sort long after they had shown the first signs of an arcus senilis. A year ago, he had surprised everyone by passing his ophthalmological diploma at the sixth and, by the rules, final attempt.

He does not respond to the pleasantries quite as I expected him to. Is this old, plodding seriousness the result of not being quite attuned to the twists and turns of social situations whose foreignness may have attenuated over the years but never entirely disappeared? Or is it a symptom of a bottomlesss preoccupation with something that cuts through all pleasantries – the ultimate anti-pleasantry of death? Whatever its cause, it makes this first meeting with our dying colleague more awkward than one might expect it to be.

As to the fact that he *is* dying, there can be no doubt. Sister has already whispered how pale he looks ('though it is difficult to tell with someone with dark skin') and how much weight he has lost; and I have contributed the observation that he seemed rather short of breath when he came in. And we all know the diagnosis. And so does he. And the prognosis. And so does he. He knows that he is dying. He must also know when – to the nearest few months, at any rate – he will stop dying. It is probable that in the distant past he had to answer an examination question on the disease of which he is now dying. He earned extra marks, perhaps, for remembering the rarer complications. He must therefore be fully aware that the events of next summer will not concern him. And he will be able to hazard a few highly-informed guesses as to how he will die. In the early hours of the morning in his solitary hospital flat, he will imagine where the metastases are going to lodge. For he knows how little islands of cells can nest in the bones and flood the whole world with a pain in which, as the hours slow to centuries, he will drown. He knows how bits of the lungs that have brought him oxygen and life will colonise his brain, erode his memory, unhinge his actions from the reasons and impulses or lack of reasons and lack of impulses that have hitherto governed a daily life more notable for conscientiousness than joy. How they can spread throughout the body and expel all the small happinesses and large worries, all the concerns, all the normal weariness, that has until this year made up its quota of quotidian sense. He knows that within a very few months he will be fighting for his breath and losing; wandering the streets or his flat, or his bedroom or his bed or his mind, in a muddle of aches and voices; crawling the barbed route leading from self-conscious existence, via a sentient body immobilised by anaemia and cachexia, into non-being.

He lowers himself into the seat behind his desk, as if he were an over-filled cup being served. Is it because he is afraid of dislodging a clump of metastatic cells – cells that will drive a slow knife of multiplication through his liver or his spine or his brain – that he is so deliberate in his movements? Or has his thoracotomy wound trained him in the art of gentle movement by rewarding careless ones with a vivid rehearsal of the scalpel's passage through his chest wall?

We exchange a few words as I borrow the spare ophthalmoscope on his desk. He makes sense of the sounds I produce; extracts from them the sense I intend through them. And this makes it all the more strange that he is soon to become an orphaned corpse – there seem to be few to mourn this lonely man – as inert and as deaf as an orange or a brick or an ophthalmoscope. Speech will cease to resonate in his head as meaning; light falling on his eyes will no longer be a seen world surrounding him.

For the present, however, the coming senselessness is held off. The world this Monday morning (the first of an unnumbered few) is still open to him and he to it. Its moments are filled with meaningful light and meaningful sound, woven into an unbroken fabric of significance, of intelligibility extending in all directions towards never-to-be-completed understanding. Its instants each contain their tiny recesses of futurity (fashioned out of hints drawn from all the corners of the earth) hollowed out in his mind by things like me that surround him. He knows where he is and what he is about. Mr Rees, Sister and I still make sense to him. There is still light; there is still meaning; he is still alive.

There is still the next patient, work to be done, the Clinic to be got through by lunch-time.

> [Lydgate] had two selves within him apparently, and they must learn to accommodate each other and bear reciprocal impediments. Strange, that some of us, with quick alternate vision, see beyond our infatuations, and even while we rave on the heights, behold the wide plain where our persistent self pauses and awaits us.
>
> George Eliot, *Middlemarch*

A Poem by
Susan Fox

Conspiracy of One

Old Mr. Iskowitz
had visitors the thirtieth of April.
Next day he disappeared.
Six nurses, three guards, and two officials of the nursing home
spent half the day searching.
At dinnertime old Mr. Iskowitz, pajama-clad,
was spotted climbing slowly
out of the IRT.
He looked confused.

The day dawned gloomy, though the sun was out by noon.
Sol didn't care. His day had nothing to do with weather.
Purpose reminded him
of a tiny stash of coins,
of train routes,
of gestures that would override
his faded hospital pajamas.
The trick, he told himself,
veteran of countless civil conflicts,
is in the eyes:
Look straight ahead like straight ahead is right.
All the way down from the North Bronx
he looked straight ahead.
Headlines, punkers, babies in slings,
the man with a ferret in his shirt,
begged his attention
but Sol held firm. Straight ahead. He knew the trick.

He remembered to get off carefully at Union Square,
waiting for the moving grate to meet the train.
That was all that matched his memory.
On the corner where Kleins Department Store once stood
three cranes herded a construction site.
Okay, so why should Kleins get richer?

But cranes that high? As high as towers,
as high as flight.
That's it! thought Sol –
all his ninety years of dreams
invested in a world
where cranes did the work
so workers could be free –
We did it! It's begun!

Vindicated, festive, he was ready for the drums.
Holiday rolls – he loved the sound.
Bullhorns. Anthems. Chants.
Jeers, okay, but who'd mind jeers
on a day like this?
His spine recalled its length,
his eyes their color –
his slippered feet rehearsed the march.
He looked around for comrades.
None that he knew, of course –
those were all dead,
or turned,
or, like his visitors the day before,
aged into wistfulness
('Tomorrow, Solly, you know what tomorrow is?'
Benny had asked,
and Sol had made himself remember: May Day).
New brothers he looked for, young ones,
with dreams as far beyond his own
as those three cranes surpassed
the creaking wobblers of his day.

The park was calm.
Sol strained for sound: traffic.
The stubby walls of the Square,
postered and sprayed with decades of graffiti,
were down. Half the trees were gone.
A swirled mosaic plaza replaced the speaker's post.
Cold took Sol's throat,
more sweat than he'd felt in twenty years
froze down his sides.
Benny said today! It's May Day!
Then this isn't Union Square!
Wrong train, wrong station –

old man, stupid, missed the stop – ask!
'Yeah man Union Square – spare change?'
(too stoned to see the old man sag in his pajamas) –
Sol asked again, a woman: He was here.
Then where was May Day?
Ten solid hours of speeches, fanfares, hymns –
where?
No drum to time his step,
Sol shuffled through the Square, the bastion,
now just a pretty urban park. Nothing.
Exhausted, he sat down.
Two girls eating out of cardboard boxes
moved down the bench to give him room.
The smell of food repelled him.
Cold wrought iron stung.
Fool, idiot, he chanted to himself.
They moved it, and you didn't even know.
An excursion you've had.
You took a little trip.
Idiot. Moron. Jerk.

Hours he sat there. The sun began to fade.
He shivered. He remembered the cardboard boxes of food.
He watched people crossing the park to somewhere.
He rehearsed the route to the Bronx,
but the fare coming down was ten times what he'd thought
and he'd spent his coins.
Okay, so die here, jerk –
freeze to a bench in Union Square.
Poetic justice.
No. Pathetic. Sol gathered himself and rose.
A middle-aged woman in a fur-trimmed leather coat
eyed his pajamas and his terry scuffs.
He felt like a starved wet dog,
wanted to snarl, wanted to move on. Couldn't.
Muttered: trainfare.
Took it. Left.

Someone gave him a seat. The car was warm.
Moron. Fool.
All the way home to the North Bronx
old Mr. Iskowitz reviled himself
for missing his last parade.

Poetry not Prozac

Jane Davis talks to Robin Philipp

Tell me about your early life. You are a New Zealander; how did you come to be a doctor here in the UK, and interested in the health-giving potential of poetry?
My parents were married here in England, then they emigrated to New Zealand and I was born and brought up there. My father was a general practitioner. He graduated from Bristol and went into practice there, but had very bad asthma, so my parents decided to emigrate from the foggy damp weather, and from the moment they arrived in New Zealand, his health improved dramatically. I came over here in 1973 as a postgraduate student to study preventive medicine. I'd worked for four and a half years as a junior doctor in New Zealand in general medicine and in paediatrics, and I found that my interests were becoming focused on what can we do to help people stay well, rather than waiting until they became ill and then doing something about it. What is implied by the concept of 'dis-ease' began to intrigue me more and more. Nowadays, having moved in 1996 from my Consultant Senior Lecturership in the University of Bristol to work as a full-time consultant NHS occupational physician, I estimate that some 70% of my clinical case-load is patients with emotional disorders.

Most of us have an emotional disorder of some sort, don't we? None of us are perfect, or have perfectly formed or perfectly survived lives. Is ill health – dis-ease, as you called it – just veering over the edge of that scale, as it were?
Yes, I think there is a spectrum of this, and to some extent we all have anxieties, things in life that we actually have to face; the point at which they become abnormal rather than a variation of normal is a very hard one to judge, and a very personal one. The estimate in Western countries is that one in four or one in five of us will at some point experience a psychological disorder – meaning mostly anxiety or depression – sufficiently severe to send us to our doctor seeking help; and the cost nowadays of managing those disorders is something that's attracting a huge amount of interest. The annual direct costs in terms of prescribing the SSRI group of anti-depressants medications, like Prozac, are enormous: in the UK in 1992 they were

£81 million. I'm interested in taking further some of the cost-benefit work that we have done in this area, looking at activities like reading and writing, particularly with poetry. I'm not saying it's suitable for everyone, but we've estimated that the annual health-care prescribing cost savings from turning to poetry instead of using antidepressants in this country could be as much as about £1.8 million.

There's been a huge amount of media interest in your work...
When we published the first Nuffield Trust report in 1999 there was a huge amount of interest. We initially asked the question in the *British Medical Journal*, in 1994: could or does reading or writing poetry benefit health? To my surprise I was deluged with comment. When I analysed the responses, I found that of those people, about two thirds felt that reading poetry helped them personally by their being able to identify with the theme, subject matter, or the mood or the rhythm of the poem; about two thirds felt that they had benefited from writing poetry, by its acting as a form of emotional catharsis for them – a sort of getting off their chests of feelings and worries that they had.

Most people would not be surprised about the writing element. I'd guess that more than 50% of the population write some form of poetry spontaneously when they are distressed or confused. But what about reading poetry? I really don't think that's recognised in the same way. It is much less obvious to a lay person that reading would have the same kind of cathartic effect as writing.
Not so much a cathartic effect; it was more linked with the affirmation of oneself. When reading a poem, somebody might be thinking: 'This is how I feel. Somebody else has experienced this. I'm relieved to find I'm not the only one. The metaphor and the imagery this writer is using – I can identify with that.' These were the sorts of comments we were hearing, after that initial question we posed in the *BMJ*. People told us of a sense of release and relief.

But how did all this get going for you?
At the Cheltenham Festival of Literature in October 1993, there was a lecture given by Danny Abse, who is a doctor and a poet, on John Keats. I went to that and was mightily intrigued by something Danny Abse quoted from Keats. He had apparently asked the question: 'Do we at times retreat from the reality of the external environment into ourselves, or do we at times retreat from the outer environment into the reality of our inner selves?' I was reminded in this of what the philosopher Epictetus, who I think lived in about the fourth century BC, said: 'Men are disturbed not by things, but by the views that they take of them.' Those were the two key things that got me thinking more

and more about poetry and health. I'm sure it was also linked to my own family background, both to my father and the way he practised medicine, and to my mother's work in social welfare and her strong interest in and understanding of English literature – she had some of her own poetry published. Following that, together with a psychiatrist and a GP, who both shared my interests, we then had a small qualitative study published in *The Lancet* (February 1996). It looked at the first 196 members of the general public who had spontaneously contacted me following the news media interest: 7% of them said that they'd been able to be weaned off tranquillisers or anti-depressants, by their GP, as a consequence of reading or writing poetry. That was what really fired me up to think a little bit more around all of this.

What's come of all that interest?

From that, initially one humanities academic, and then about four or five poetry professionals contacted me, and said: 'Look, might we try and do something with all of this?' People were coming from psychology and counselling, nursing, medicine and other health professions, from English literature and from adult education. Out of that, in 1996 we started LAPIDUS. It now has some 350 members, Arts Council funding, a full-time administrator and it covers all the literary arts. Every year there is a national conference; this year it was on the theme of journeys. LAPIDUS has now consolidated a lot of interest in this area of the arts and humanities in health and well-being, and one of the exciting things has been the inter-disciplinarity of its work.

Out of the work of the Nuffield Trust there have been several initiatives. Firstly there's been the journal *Medical Humanities*. Secondly there has been a new initiative of the Arts Council of England and the Department of Health, which is called 'Cultural Medicine'. The Department of Health has commissioned a strategic review of the arts and health, and the Nuffield Trust seed-funded what's called CAHHM, The Centre for Arts and Humanities in Health and Medicine, based at the University of Durham under the directorship of Dr Jane MacNaughton. Jane is a Senior Lecturer in General Practice, who moved from Glasgow to take up that work, alongside – I think he's a sculptor by background – Mike White. Mike and Jane have been doing a great deal to strengthen understanding and interest in the humanities and the arts as they apply to health and medicine. At the University College Hospital, London, Professor Mike Baum was particularly instrumental in seeding the development for what has now become the UCL Centre for Medical Humanities, and Deborah Kirklin is the director there. They host an annual conference in the arts and humanities at UCL, which has been very successful.

These all feel like very ground-breaking new developments that have happened over the last ten, maybe fifteen years. **But if I were to go to a hospital or my GP and ask for some practical help, is there anything that will have been affected? Is medical humanities touching patients, in any way?**

Yes, there is a change in the quality of the environment in some instances, and in terms of arts-based activities going on in hospital and primary care environments. In terms of what's going on in general practices, the leading light in that was Malcolm Rigler, who was a GP based at Withymoor in the West Midlands. He wanted to foster, in what was then a newly-built housing estate area, a welcoming environment where people living in the area could feel they could meet in the General Practice setting and engage with community-based activities. One of their first projects was to have a Poet in Residence set up there, and that worked extremely well. Not only did that poet help to relax people who were waiting in the waiting room, encouraging them to think about imagery and metaphor, but he also helped them in other ways, with, for example, support in writing their own letters and how to complete a Curriculum Vitae, quite practical supportive activities that would help people with their own ability to move on a bit in life. From that, and one or two other pilots that were set up very much on a local basis, through the interests of other individual General Practitioners, the Poetry Society in London developed and funded a Poets in Residence scheme, supporting a number of people in different parts of the country. One that got to be very well known about was here in Bedminster, an area of central Bristol.

Yes, I've heard of this.

The General Practitioner there who was very interested in setting something up in Bristol was Dr Gillian Rice. The Poetry Society scheme funded Rose Flint, a poet who is also a qualified Art Therapist, to work in her practice. Rose had a lot of success with individual patients, by working with them principally on confidence, self-esteem and morale. One of my own patients was actually a patient of Gillian's practice, and found that by going to Rose's classes, it helped her own outlook on herself, such that she felt motivated to do something about herself and her own appearance. That was the way she began to tackle her obesity and Type 2 diabetes; emotionally she felt she benefited considerably. Whether the benefits of this approach are long term is difficult to know, because long-term follow-ups are difficult to undertake. The write-up evaluating the project did however demonstrate that it really was very successful. The Poetry Society funded a number of other Poets in Residence opportunities, not just in General Practices, but in hospital environments, libraries, schools and some workplaces. I don't know whether those schemes are on-going, but out of this initiative came others such as 'Poems in the Waiting Room', which are equally successful.

What are the difficulties of the poetry and health projects?
The Wellcome Foundation organised a meeting, probably about ten years ago now, to discuss ways forward for the arts and health in healthcare environments, and the audience rapidly fell into two groups: the artists, who were saying 'This is what we do, and we know it helps because people tell us it does'; and the healthcare purchasers, who were saying 'Look, it sounds fantastic, but where's the evidence?' At that stage, the artists didn't seem to like the scientific model, and the healthcare purchasers wouldn't buy in to the artistic way of looking at their work. So to try and help explain the links and establish a framework that could take the debate forward, in a book that was published by Jessica Kingsley in 1997, called *The Arts and Healthcare: A Palette of Possibilities*, I was asked to write the chapter called 'Evaluating the Effectiveness of the Arts in Healthcare', which looked at the aims and objectives of arts and humanities in healthcare; how and why the arts can help; how we evaluate arts projects in healthcare; and how we build a practical approach to research and development.

I think that we've passed that stage now, and these days the arts practitioners do fully appreciate the need to evaluate. The difficulty now is in finding people who have got the time to write well-structured interdisciplinary research protocols of high scientific quality, but which are able at the same time to address what can sometimes be seen as a fairly woolly arts-based question. If we get the funding for it, we're about to start a randomised controlled trial to look at the role of some eight to ten weekly poetry workshops in helping cancer patients with their emotional resilience and coping skills. The study design has taken a long time to pull together in a robust way with well validated research methods, such that patients, clinicians and poetry therapists are happy with it.

Will people select themselves onto that trial?
It has to be to some extent self-selected. Probably we will offer it to all people with certain types of cancers, not just cancer generally, so that it's a bit purer in its research design. But the oncologists in Bristol are very interested, as are some of the surgeons, and to have them interested and motivated is fantastic. Going back to your point 'Well, if I went to my GP what might she or he say?', we are finding now that there are an increasing number who use these sorts of ideas to support individuals, for example in establishing rapport

and empathy with patients and with intuitive understanding of what patients are seeking to convey. For example, one might say something like 'It seems to me that this' – say, Rudyard Kipling's poem 'If' – 'says something of what you are talking about; does it feel like that to you?', or W.H. Davies' poem 'Leisure', 'What is this life if, full of care, / We have no time to stand and stare'. I sometimes use that one in particular as one way of saying to people, 'Look, this is nature's way of saying you've got to get off the treadmill for a bit, stop at the bus stop and let the buses go by.' There, I'm doing it again, I'm using another form of imagery or of metaphor. It seems to me however that when I use that sort of approach, patients can identify with it more readily, it dawns on them for themselves in their own ways, and I can then help them to reinforce their own models of thinking, such that they can come to understand why there is turmoil in their own mind, and then be willing to actually start to work with understanding it, clarifying the issues and restructuring approaches to them.

It's interesting in relation to, say, cognitive behavioural therapy. As somebody who has had therapy, and has had a literary education, I can't help but think, CBT is great, you know, if it really is teaching you to think about things, but what you need to think well as a human being is a complex language. In a way, that's what you're saying over and over again with metaphor, imagery, and so on. If you read self-help books, or even positive psychology books, the language is thin compared to the language of poetry or literature, though the ideas are often similar. In a way what you're saying is 'I want, as a doctor, access to a very complex kind of language, a kind of tool-kit if you like, for being a human being.'
I think it's not so much a tool-kit as opening people's minds to tools that we have all got access to, but perhaps we've never really thought about, and we've not been sure how to use them. I agree with you, I think that the analogy with CBT is very exciting, and it is a form of self-help to build up a resource for yourself. But it goes back to our individual ways of looking at things, and how we each use those tools, or how we even become aware that they are there. People are picking up on this; if we look at the special study modules in the undergraduate medical curriculum, some of these are for example based around literature.

We've just set one up at Liverpool. I'm looking forward to working with medical students.
So that will mean that people are coming out of medical school, going into General Practice gradually, and will have these tools in their mind as part of their interior armoury. The difficulty for the

GPs in applying these sorts of methods is that the average GP consultation is 8–10 minutes, and in 8–10 minutes you cannot get into this sort of thing in any depth or detail, and you certainly can't just say 'Go and read a good book, you'll feel better'.

I agree that it's a growing thing, and that things have really changed over the last ten years, but in a way, that's changed because there are a few individuals like yourself making that change happen, so why you? Why are you doing this? You've told me a bit about your family stuff, so tell me a bit about your reading life.
[laughs] With this much writing I don't get much time to do any reading! Just for fun, last night I thought, what are the sorts of books that I treasure and read?, so I pulled them out. Most of these fall into a group, which is about people who are thinkers and philosophers. *Voltaire's Bastards* by John Ralston Saul is one, Theodore Zeldin's *An Intimate History of Humanity* is another, *Sophie's World* by Jostein Gaarder… A slightly different one is Isabel Allende, the niece of the former president of Chile, which is one that my father recommended to me, and which I particularly loved. I don't read that many novels. It's mostly a time thing, because the job here that I've got, when I'm not seeing patients, is researching and writing, and when I'm not writing, I'm reading journals and thinking about the writing to be done. I do too, in my day-to-day work, have to read an enormous amount of medical literature to keep up to date.

Do you read poetry?
I particularly enjoy some of the Romantics. But the first poem I ever had to learn at school was W.B. Yeats' 'The Lake Isle of Innisfree'. Although we studied it at school, it never really had a proper impact on me until I came to London and started walking those 'pavements grey', because I was then in my mind's eye thinking through what it is Yeats must have thought. For me coming from New Zealand, my own little bit of heaven on earth 12,000 miles from here had, I thought, to somehow remain in my mind's eye. The poem allowed me to retreat when I needed to into that headspace – and at times I still do so!

Thank you for taking the time to talk to *The Reader*.

A short biography about Robin and more information about his work is available on the Arts Access International website: www.artsaccessinternational.org

Two Poems by
Jen Hadfield

The Screen Door

The screen door catches my heels
when it swings shut,
like that needy kind of dog
that's always round your ankles.
Bang! And the tattered flyscreen shivers.

My life at its best
is compulsively bursting out of houses
and making robins stand tall
on the lawn in their waistcoats,
bellies stuck out like the Skating Parson.

And what now? The mountain,
that mountain, the bulky cone
of my mountain, cuts a chevron
into the sky. And all at once
how good the air is. It swirls
in lazy backwash like batter

smelling like beeswax, at odds
with tweed of mulch, moss and rain.
You have to sift it through you.
Hang it round your face
in a swaying nosebag. Dig your hand
in a cool sack of seed,
dislodging an avalanche of slippery grain.

Thirty Years Back, in the Cariboo

Moira had a frog in a stranglehold
and James, a skinny kid,
crushed the sides of his cowboy hat
against his head.
His belly was sticking out
and his spine shoved in, relaxed
but strung, a sapling bow.
Arched, the shape of his torso.
Grandmere highstepped a creek.
Binoculars clappered her chest
and her arms were full. Four cagoules
and a besom of pussywillow.
And your plaid shirt
spanned your stomach and hung straight
from belt to collarbone, bright as a banner,
arterial red and vascular blue.
Snow huddled under some of the pines
like lambs: shrinking, wet and wrung.
The winter grass was yellow,
but beginning to sour and brighten
and faces were as yellow
as gouda moons.
The grass was just turning,
thirty years back, in the Cariboo.

The Shakespeared Brain

Philip Davis

in collaboration with Neil Roberts,
Victorina González-Díaz and Guillaume Thierry

I have always been very interested in how literature affects us. But I don't really like it when people say, 'This book changed my life!' Struggling with ourselves and our seemingly inextricable mixture of strengths and weaknesses, surely we know that change is much more difficult and much less instant than that. It does scant justice to the deep nature of a life to suppose that a book can simply 'change' it. Literature is not a one-off remedy. And actually it is the reading of books itself, amongst other things, that has helped me appreciate that deep complex nature. Nonetheless, I do remain convinced that life without reading and the personal thinking it provokes would be a greatly diminished thing. So, with these varying considerations, I know I need to think harder about what literature does.

And here's another thing. In the last few years I have become interested not only in the contents of the thoughts I read – their meaning for me, their mental and emotional effect – but also in the very *shapes* these thoughts take; a shape inseparable, I feel, from that content.

Moreover, I had a specific intuition – about Shakespeare: that the very shapes of Shakespeare's lines and sentences somehow had a dramatic effect at deep levels in my mind. For example – Macbeth at the end of his tether:

> And that which should accompany old age,
> As honour, love, obedience, troops of friends,
> I must not look to have, but in their stead
> Curses, not loud but deep, mouth-honour, breath
> Which the poor heart would fain deny and are not.

It simply would not be the same, would it, if Shakespeare had written it out more straightforwardly: I must not look to have the honour, love, obedience, troops of friends which should accompany old age. Nor would it be the same if he had not suddenly coined that disgusted phrase 'mouth-honour' (now a cliché as 'lip-service').

I took this hypothesis – about grammatical or linear shapes and their mapping onto shapes *inside* the brain – to a scientist, Professor Neil Roberts who heads MARIARC (the Magnetic Resonance and Image Analysis Research Centre) at the University of Liverpool. In particular I mentioned to him the linguistic phenomenon in Shakespeare which is known as 'functional shift' or 'word class conversion'. It refers to the way that Shakespeare will often use one part of speech – a noun or an adjective, say – to serve as another, often a verb, shifting its grammatical nature with minimal alteration to its shape. Thus in *Lear* for example, Edgar comparing himself to the king: 'He *childed* as I *fathered*' (nouns shifted to verbs); in *Troilus and Cressida*, '*Kingdomed* Achilles in commotion rages' (noun converted to adjective); Othello 'To *lip* a *wanton* in a secure couch/And to suppose her chaste!' (noun 'lip' to verb; adjective 'wanton' to noun). The effect is often electric I think, like a lightning-flash in the mind: for this is an economically compressed form of speech, as from an age when the language was at its most dynamically fluid and formatively mobile; an age in which a word could move quickly from one sense to another, in keeping with Shakespeare's lightning-fast capacity for forging metaphor. It was a small example of sudden change of shape, of concomitant effect upon the brain. Could we make an experiment out of it?

We decided to try to *see* what happens inside us when the brain comes upon sentences such as 'The dancers *foot* it with grace', or 'We waited for *disclose* of news', or 'Strong wines *thick* my thoughts', or 'I could *out-tongue* your griefs' or 'Fall down and *knee*/The way into his mercy'. For research suggests that there is one specific part of the brain that processes nouns and another part that processes verbs: but what happens when for a micro-second there is a serious hesitation between whether, in context, this is noun or verb? The main cognitive research done so far on the confusion of verbs and nouns has been to do with mistakes made by those who are brain-damaged and thus on the possible neural correlates of grammatical errors and semantic violations. Hardly anybody appears to have investigated the neural processing of a 'positive error' such as functional shift in normal healthy organisms. This truly would be a small instance of inner drama.

We decided to experiment using three pieces of kit. First, EEG (electroencephalogram) tests, with electrodes placed on different parts of the scalp to measure brain-events taking place in time; then MEG (magnetoencephalograhy), a helmet-like brain-scanner which measures effects in terms of location in the brain as well as their timing; and finally fMRI (functional magnetic resonance imaging), those tunnel-like brain-scanners which focus even more specifically on brain-activation by location. I knew nothing much of this: I am indebted to Professor Roberts and to Dr Guillaume Thierry of Bangor University who joined us in the enterprise. With the help of my colleague in English language, Victorina González-Díaz, as well as the scientists, I designed a set of stimuli – 40 examples of Shakespeare's functional shift. At this very early and rather primitive stage, we could not give our student-subjects undiluted lines of Shakespeare because too much in the brain would light up in too many places: that is one of the definitions of what Shakespeare-language does. So, the stimuli we created were simply to do with the noun-to-verb or verb-to-noun shift-words themselves, with more ordinary language around them. It is not Shakespeare taken neat; it is just based on Shakespeare, with water. But around each of those sentences of functional shift we also provided three counter-examples which were shown on screen to the experiment's subjects in random order: all they had to do was press a button saying whether the sentence roughly made sense or not. Thus below A ('accompany') is a sentence which is conventionally grammatical, makes simple sense, and acts as a control; B ('charcoal') is grammatically odd, like a functional shift, but it makes no semantic sense in context; C ('incubate') is grammatically correct but still semantically does not make sense; D ('companion') is a Shakespearian functional shift from noun to verb, and is grammatically odd but does make sense:

A) I was not supposed to go there alone: you said you would *accompany* me.
B) I was not supposed to go there alone: you said you would *charcoal* me.
C) I was not supposed to go there alone: you said you would *incubate* me.
D) I was not supposed to go there alone: you said you would *companion* me.

What happened to our subjects' brains when they read the critical words (on screen in front of them but not italicised in our experiments)?

So far we have just carried out the EEG stage of experimentation under Dr Thierry at Bangor.

EEG works as follows in its graph-like measurements. When the brain senses a semantic violation (i.e. 'This sentence does not seem to make sense!'), it automatically registers what is called an N400 effect, a negative wave modulation 400 milliseconds after the onset of the critical word that disrupts the meaning of a sentence. The N400 amplitude is small when little semantic integration effort is needed (e.g., to integrate the word 'eat' in the sentence 'the pizza was too hot to eat'), and large when the critical word is unexpected and therefore difficult to integrate (e.g., 'the pizza was too hot to *sing*').

But when the brain senses a syntactic violation (i.e. 'This sentence is not grammatical!'), there is a P600 effect, a parietal modulation peaking approximately 600 milliseconds after the onset of the word that upsets syntactic integrity. Thus, when a word violates the grammatical structure of a sentence (e.g., 'the pizza was too hot to *mouth*'), a positive going wave is systematically observed.

Preliminary results suggest this:

(A) With the simple control sentence ('you said you would *accompany* me'), NO N400 or P600 effect because it is correct both semantically and syntactically.

(B) With 'you said you would *charcoal* me', BOTH N400 and P600 highs, because it violates both grammar and meaning.

(C) With 'you said you would *incubate* me', NO P600 (it makes grammatical sense) but HIGH N400 (it makes no semantic sense).

(D) With the Shakespearian 'you said you would *companion* me', HIGH P600 (because it feels like a grammatical anomaly) but NO N400 (the brain will tolerate it, almost straightaway, as making sense despite the grammatical difficulty). This is in marked contrast with B above.

So what? First, it was as Guillaume Thierry had predicted. It meant that 'functional shift' was a robust phenomenon: that is to say, it had a distinct and unique effect on the brain. Instinctively Shakespeare was right to use it as one of his dramatic tools.

Second, and more surprisingly, the P600 effect continued *after* the word ('companion') that triggered it. The brain was thus primed to look out for more difficulty, to work at a higher level, whilst still accepting that fundamental sense was being made. In other words, while the Shakespearian functional shift was semantically integrated with ease, it triggered a syntactic re-evaluation process likely to raise attention and give more weight to the sentence as a whole. Shakespeare is stretching us; he is opening up the possibility of further peaks, new potential pathways or developments. Our findings show how Shakespeare created dramatic effects by *implicitly* taking advantage of the relative independence – *at the neural level* – of semantics and syntax in sentence comprehension. It is as though he is a pianist using one hand to keep the background melody going, whilst simultaneously the other pushes towards ever more complex variations and syncopations.

This is a small beginning. But it has some importance in the development of inter-disciplinary studies – the cooperation of arts and sciences in the study of the mind, the brain, and the neural inner processing of language felt as an experience of excitement, never fully explained or exhausted by subsequent explanation or conceptualisation. It is that neural excitement that gets to me: those peaks of sudden pre-conscious understanding coming into consciousness itself; those possibilities of shaking ourselves up at deep, momentary levels of being.

This, then, is a chance to map something of what Shakespeare does to mind at the level of brain, to catch the flash of lightning that makes for thinking. For my guess, more broadly, remains this: that Shakespeare's syntax, its shifts and movements, can lock into the existing pathways of the brain and actually move and change them – away from old and ageing mental habits and easy long-established sequences. It could be that Shakespeare's use of language gets so far into our brains that he shifts and new-creates pathways – not unlike the establishment of new biological networks using novel combinations of existing elements (genes/proteins in biology: units of phonology, semantics, syntax, and morphology in language). Then indeed we might be able to see something of the ways literature can cause affect or create change, without resorting to being assertively gushy.

I do not think this is reductive. Cognitive science is often to do with the discovery of the precise localisation of functions. But suppose that instead we can show the following by neuro-imaging: that for all the localisation of noun-processing in one place and the localisation of verb-processing in another, when the brain is asked to work at more complex meanings, the localisation gives way to the *movement between* the two static locations. Then the brain is working at a higher level of evolution, at an emergent consciousness paradoxically *un*determined by the structures it *still* works from. And then we might be re-discovering at a demonstrable neural level the experience not merely of specialist 'art' but of thinking itself going on not in static terms but in dynamic ones. At present there is of course no brain imaging system that allows the study of continuous thought. But the hope is that, within experimental limitations, we might be able to gain a glimpse within ourselves of a changing neurological configuration of the brain, like the shape of the syntax just ahead of the realisation of the semantics.

In that case Shakespeare's art would be no more and no less than the supreme example of a mobile, creative and adaptive human capacity, in deep relation between brain and language. It makes new combinations, creates new networks, with changed circuitry and added levels, layers and overlaps. And all the time it works like the cry of 'action' on a film-set, by sudden peaks of activity and excitement dramatically breaking through into consciousness. It makes for what William James said of mind in his *Principles of Psychology*, 'a theatre of simultaneous possibilities'. This could be a new beginning to thinking about reading and mental changes.

Broken Plate

Karen King-Aribisala

The widowed women, wedded in sorrow, draw close together; widows together. Gathering on this tight night they try to shut out the fears and the doubts of their hearts. One of them, the one who has called them to this gathering, breaks a plate.

Such a simple thing... the breaking of a plate. This widow is from a certain part of Nigeria. She refuses to tell the other widows which part, which region she comes from. This widow thinks that such things are unimportant. And so she breaks the plate. The breaking of the plate is not done to draw attention to herself. She breaks the plate because she has chosen to break it with her own hands. She breaks the plate at this time because when her husband died she was told as custom demanded that she a widow should break a plate and eat her food on the pieces of broken plate to mourn for her dead husband. She refused and refusing again was beaten until she bled.

The widow points at the broken pieces of plate.

Pieces of broken plate on the floor far away from prying, condemning eyes. In this abandoned building no one can see them, hear them, the widows. But widowed eyes see and widowed ears hear and widows' hearts try to prevent themselves from breaking again as they have been broken.

The widows. The pieces. The broken plate. Some might say it is a prating plate, its clattering sound, the idle chatter of women. The widows believe and want to believe it is a talk-discussing plate. A turning round of situation plate. A gluing of things together after they have been broken kind of plate.

Talk Broken Plate Talk:

'When my husband passed away...'

'Go ahead, continue. Don't stop. The time for tears is over. Speak. Our meeting here will change things. We widows have gone through a lot – everywhere in every part of this our Nigeria – we have rights, after tonight we'll do something. We'll change things. Speak.'

'They shaved me. They shaved me with a broken bottle... not, not only my head.' She removes her scarf, reveals the bald wound of her naked head, tissued in laceration.

'They did it here too. No! I want to show you what they did!'

Her wrapper falls to the floor. Her hands move downward – deft, urgent – pulling at her clothes under. And though the widows have heard with their ears of this, when they see the skin with its network of swelling sores they do not want to see or hear.

'I'm grateful that you looked, saw it... I...'

She reties her wrapper.

'I kept my eyes closed the whole time they did it. Afterwards they gave me the hair... my pubic hair... I put it in... I kept it. I don't know why but I kept it.'

Shaven. Shaven to show respect for her dead husband.

Broken Plate Speak:

'Na wa for my people oh! I no fit speak grammar I beg. Forgive me-oh! I nearly vomit when my husband people dem come my house, take me go im village and wash my husband corpse im body, hand, leg... dem pour water, dem squeeze water from sponge and put for calabash and make me say drink am. I say no. I no gree drink dead water. I go sick if I drink am. They say if I no drink am I be witch. That I poison my husband and I go show dem say I no be witch. I tell them say I no be witch-oh! I no kill my husband. How I fit kill my husband? I am born am eight pickin. How I go be witch? Dem say dem go trouble me except I drink dead water. And I too tire, I get nobody wey go help me-oh and I drink the water. I vomit. Dem say if I no be witch I no suppose to vomit the water. As dem day de talk one kind man say I no look like witch.'

'Which part of the country do you come from?'

Broken Plate speak:

'I didn't have to do anything so disgusting as... God! Drinking the water which they used to wash your husband's corpse... but although my husband died many years ago I can still remember the day my in-laws came. It was a big fight I can tell you. We owned – my husband and I – we owned a business. We put into it not only money – we always had a joint account you see – we put in time, effort, energy. The business belonged to both of us, you see... No sooner had the news been broken – of his death I mean, than – I call it his village – his relatives descended. They even chartered lorries for the trip. Can you believe it? Lorries! To cart away our belongings. I'd just come home after dealing with the funeral arrangements – and it was terrible. Loss upon loss. They took the TV, video, fridge, furniture, my husband's clothing, my jewellery – everything gone – the carpet too. I chartered a taxi to their village and they were so brazen! They told me I only had those possessions because of the wealth of my husband's business and that in actual fact the property belonged to him and now that he was dead – and that I'd probably killed him anyway… they said that now he was dead the property belonged to them… I can't tell you how angry, upset, I was. I was sort of floating between grief and shock. Those same in-laws who had stayed at our house for months on end and who I had no quarrel with did that to me… It was hell I can tell you.'

Which tribe are you from? Are you Igbo, Itsekiri, Canuri, Yoruba?

The windows look at the floor and at the broken pieces of plate; scattered. It is scattered. Its edges sharp.

'Thank God my husband made a will and insisted that we sign both our names for the property. Some of my in-laws wanted to contest the will, but they gave up. If it hadn't been for that will I would be penniless today. Imagine… I used to feed those very people.'

Do you eat amala and ewedu in your part of the country or ugbonna soup?

Broken Plate Speak:
'I, I'm sorry, I, I, I, had to stay with the corpse in the death chamber. Yes, that was what it was, a death chamber. Everyone insisted that I do it. They tied my leg to the bed. And then I had to stay there. It's a miracle to me today that I didn't die. Two deaths. Two corpses. It was just me with the corpse in the room.'

Her eyes dart this way and that. 'You, I recognise you – aren't you my, my late husband's sister? You were there when they forced me to sleep in the death chamber!'

'We have suffered, but it is our tradition. I've heard that some wives treat their in-laws badly and that's why they take it out on them when their husbands die.'

Voices of Broken Plate Speaking:
'We must respect our culture.'
'You know things like what happened to us happen in America and Europe.'
'Being shaven isn't the horror you make it out to be.'

Broken Plate Speak:
Another Widow.
She speaks of days and nights in a hut in the bush with only a fire, its flames licking her in hope of an alive-warmth now dead; stoking the fire to keep her husband's spirit alive in widow vigil.

Her dirty body unwashed, her uncombed hair uncombed until the night-walking ritual of cleansing bath in the forest dark, cleansing her from a dirt ritually agreed upon is hers; that is required; that is, hers and hers only.

And she speaks of the broken plate, dirty, from which she must eat and from which she must resist its beguiling sharp-edged-edgedness which beckons 'Come cut your skin with me, break like I am broken. Take up this piece of my plateness and cut your vein in the throb where it pulsing throbs and join him, your husband in the grave. You are worthless; without the worth of your husband's life which gave you meaning. You are, if not dead, you are as dead. Dead.'

'I broke that plate at the beginning of the meeting... I broke it because, I wanted to show...'

Is your name Ngozi, Shade, Eriate, Hauwa? Which part of the country do you come from?

I do hope no one gets to know of this meeting.

They'll say we're selfish and that we don't care about our husbands' spirits.

Which tribe did you say you were from?

I hope our husbands' ghosts, our ancestors – won't come back to haunt us because of this meeting.

I'm scared. I shouldn't have come.

If we expose what we've gone through they'll say Africans are primitive.

In Europe or America widows don't have a family support system like we do in Africa.

And many of these customs are not applied today. Only in the rural areas and certainly no educated woman would put up with them.

We mustn't give our culture a bad name.

'I broke that plate because I wanted to put an end to...'

I must go home. I'll be missed. I'm sure I'll be missed.

Such a simple thing; the breaking of a plate.

I feel better for talking about it, but... I must go home.

Speak Broken Plate Speak:
I must go home... We... must... go... home... I... We...

Medicine Through the Novel

Roddy Doyle, *The Woman who Walked into Doors*
London: Vintage, 1998

This article was originally printed in the *BMJ* (June 2000)

Ann Jay

Paula Spencer, nee O'Leary, is 37 years old. She looks much older, although she might have been good-looking once. The booze and the fags have taken their toll. She has four children, one of whom is an addict. They have not been well fed, probably because the money goes on vodka, and they've all been bed-wetters. She was married to a small-time crook who managed to get himself killed by the Garda during a bungled robbery. He was a charmer, though, and handsome, always very concerned about her when she had yet another fall under the influence. He would take her to the hospital and stay with her whilst she was treated.

Paula has a thick medical record. It bulges with reports from casualty about her black eyes and broken bones. She has been to her general practitioner on numerous occasions with complaints of tiredness and depression. She has never heeded the advice to cut down on her drinking and give up smoking, even when pregnant. She's on Valium most of the time:

> 'The doctor never looked at me. He studied parts of me but he never saw all of me. He never looked at my eyes. Drink, he said to himself. I could see his nose moving, taking in the smell, deciding.'

Doctors don't like Paula very much. She could be described as a 'heartsink' patient which probably amounts to the same thing. She doesn't like them either. They have singularly failed to help her. This is put another way in a paper by Butler and Evans:

> 'Heartsink' and related terms like 'black holes', 'difficult', 'hateful' and 'health care abuser' are pejorative and it has

been suggested that doctors use them to make themselves feel better at not being able to alleviate the multifaceted suffering of these patients.[1]

Paula is, of course, a fiction, a product of Roddy Doyle's imagination, but such a rich and rounded product that I find it easy to think of her as a patient. Indeed she is so well written that it is actually quite difficult not to regard her as real. Most general practitioners know a Paula. They will meet her in the surgery and perhaps at a case conference. What they are much less likely to do is meet her at a party or as a neighbour. If they saw her in Tesco they would probably find themselves hoping she hadn't seen them.

Doyle introduces us to her in all her complexity. Through him she tells her life story. We meet the young, pretty girl who 'swooned the first time' she saw Charlo, the man she married, and we get the measure of the enormous sexual attraction between them. In the book two narratives are woven together, the happy story of Paula's life and the unhappy one. There is the story of the girl who spends most of her honeymoon in bed having a great time with Charlo, conceiving their first child, and the woman who is repeatedly beaten up and cowed by him. The bruises and broken bones, as we might readily guess, are the result, not of accidents, but of marital violence and Charlo takes her to the hospital, not out of concern for her, but to make sure she doesn't tell.

She doesn't tell and the medical staff don't ask, although she prays that they will:

> 'Ask me.
> In the hospital.
> Please, ask me.
> In the clinic.
> In the church.
> Ask me ask me ask me. Broken nose, loose teeth, cracked ribs. Ask me.'

Recent research shows that unless battered women are asked in a direct and supportive fashion about the violence they still may remain silent.[2] Why didn't they ask? Were they too busy or unaware or is it something more sinister than that? Paula Spencer was in no doubt: 'It was my little secret and they all helped me keep it'.

Feminists, notably Ehrenreich and English,[3] have long accused the medical profession of colluding in women's oppression. Illich suggests that the health professions rob people of the potential 'to deal with their human weakness, vulnerability and uniqueness in a personal and autonomous way'.[4] It is perhaps less controversial to suggest that medicine, as a product of a particular society, will reflect the mores of that society. In Dublin in the 1970s, where this story is set, unhappy women would have been unlikely to receive the help and support they needed to challenge the circumstances that made them unhappy. It is far more likely that they would have been encouraged to cope with an unsatisfactory situation by the prescription of a tranquilliser.[5] In the 1970s women were prescribed tranquillisers twice as often as men. Most advertisements for them featured women, often depicted as depressed housewives. Things have moved on since then. Doctors are now taught communication skills and our awareness of abuse is more acute. We no longer regard benzodiazepines as a panacea for all ills.

But difficult social problems presenting under the guise of illness are still very much a part of everyday general practice. How do we avoid the 'heartsink', the frustration at patients' failure to heed our advice about drinking and smoking, our incredulity at their inability to leave an abusive situation? One way is to understand them better. As Iona Heath says:

> Almost always, when I get stuck with a patient, when it begins to seem as if we are going round and round in circles, it turns out to be due to a failure of my imagination. The solution comes in seeking more detail, however small, of the reality of the patient's life. Each detail triggers new scope for the imagination, a renewed possibility of empathy and a much increased chance of the patient being heard.[6]

One way we, as doctors, can feed our imaginations is by reading fiction. When we see our 'Paulas' in the surgery we are constrained by lack of time and all the paraphernalia of our medical training, both of which encourage us to look for proper diagnoses and cures. When we read a novel we engage with the character in a different way. We can perhaps get under their skin and more fully realise how for some people 'cigarettes are sexy – they're worth the stench and the cancer', as Paula Spencer says. Reading *The Woman Who Walked Into Doors*, we are reminded not only of the power of cigarettes, but of the power of love and lust, the forces that much health education breaks its back over. And we see why it took Paula seventeen years to leave Charlo. It isn't just concern for her children, or the lack of money, support and somewhere to go, although these things matter very much. It is also that she carries on loving Charlo, she carries on having the two strands to her narrative that Roddy Doyle makes us see. Leaving Charlo means abandoning the happy narrative, false though it seems to us, and admitting that the unhappy one is the real story of her life. To give real help to people like Paula we must not just ask the right questions when they present with a 'peri-orbital haematoma' but also give them a way to rebuild a satisfactory narrative to their life.

Roddy Doyle's *The Woman Who Walked Into Doors* is a marvellous book. Reading it enables us to identify with a downtrodden, abused cleaner from Dublin and to appreciate the courage that makes her, as he does, a heroine. We see doctors and nurses through her eyes. It is a book that should be read by doctors and nurses everywhere.

1. C. Butler and M. Evans, 'The "Heartsink" Patient Revisited', *British Journal of General Practice*, 49 (1999), pp.230–33.
2. P. S. Konchak, 'Domestic Violence: A Primer for the Primary Care Physician', *Journal of the American Osteopathic Association* (Supp), 98 (1998) p.12.
3. B. Ehrenreich and D. English, *Complaints and Disorders: The Sexual Politics of Sickness*, New York: The Feminist Press, 1973.
4. I. Illich, *Limits to Medicine. Medical Nemesis: The Expropriation of Health*, London: Marion Boyars, 1976.
5. M. Hardey, *The Social Context of Health*. Buckingham: Open University Press,1998.
6. I. Heath, '"Uncertain Clarity": Contradiction, Meaning and Hope', *British Journal of General Practice*, 49 (1999); pp. 651–7.

Two Poems by
Keith Edwin Colwell

Simple Arithmetic

Nobody looks up hardly, he thought.
Unless in the bed nearest the door,
when two sunken eyes met his and smiled:
I can split an atom, release a sun from its core,
and he can't shake this thought:
nothingness cannot exist
like these two eyes exist.
If it does, then maybe only like zero,
a contradiction in terms,
which represents its own annihilation
in becoming something more
for the sake of sums, nothing else.
Just as the worm will divide my flesh
and multiply my bones, the last breath rises
to converge where what remains
is carried over, and zero is transformed.

What We Do

I catch sight of your hands
working in the light under the lamp;
your head adjusts minutely one way,
then the other,
to keep your eye on that crucial point
your fingers roll the putty round
under the darning-needle,
turning a grey worm of Milliput on a wire
into a miniature being from another world
where eye, hand, and needle-point
are timelessly absorbed.

When you notice me watching,
the expression of formidable intent
a man wears while he's rapt in intricate work
relaxes to an enigmatic smile:
though neither of us can do
what the other does well,
and the things we make
are as different as feathers and granite,
I want you to know I have been there,
and expect to arrive back at the final stop.

What Happened to the Revolution?

Harriet Gordon Getzels

China's moved on, but clearly I haven't. I'm chockablock in a traffic-jam on one of Beijing's spaghetti ring roads; it's easy enough to know where the fumes are coming from but impossible to squint our way to the exits with all the sunlit buildings of glass and steel. Seeing this glitz from the start of this trip – my first visit to China – I couldn't help asking, 'What happened to the revolution?'

'Part of the problem with China,' says Lu Bo, my translator, 'is all the levels of management people have to cope with.' We have flown an hour from Beijing to Henan Province and are driving along cornfields on our way to visit the last Maoist village in China. Lu Bo, a freelancer for international news agencies, is explaining to Aaron, a photographer, and me the bureaucracy the average peasant has had to face ever since Mao's successor instigated sweeping economic reforms in 1979. 'There are authorities in every capital of every province but every county in every province has its own capital with its own authorities, so you can imagine…' His voice breaks off because our taxi driver has once again sped to within an arm's reach of a lorry and slammed on the brakes.

In 1984 – five years after the reforms began – three thousand peasants in a village called Nanjie decided they were fed up with fending for themselves and gave all their personal property to a cadre of party bosses to manage. In exchange, they agreed to live according to Mao's Red Book and leave it to their bosses to turn new, free-market opportunities into profits that would benefit them all. Thanks in part to outside consultants who came up with the idea of a factory to make dried, instant noodles – the first in China – the people of Nanjie have a much better standard of living than their counterparts elsewhere, with free housing, heating oil, medical care, education, food, and equal wages. But I would soon learn that nothing in Nanjie is free.

After a couple hours the roadsides begin to bulge with people on rusty bicycles, rickshaws and wooden carts towed by undersized engines belching smoke. The county capital, Linying, is busy with the grime and bustle of mechanics, glaziers and iron-mongers whose wares spill from shop fronts onto the pavement. Grocers and restaurants also dot the road, topped by billboards showing smiling girls selling toothpaste or soap. We turn left and suddenly the boulevard is empty and spotlessly clean. Adverts are replaced by profiles of sunlit peasants, soldiers and workers, while colossal murals of Stalin, Marx, Lenin and Engels dominate the main roundabout. Giant red characters clutch the walls of white tile buildings, sprawling like spiders bent out of control. Lu Bo cannot read fast enough for me: 'No matter how good things are, socialism is best'; 'One man cannot achieve anything alone'; 'If you want to make progress, always learn the Mao theory'.

Aaron Deemer

If a Maoist village were going to spring up anywhere in China, it's not surprising that it happened in Henan Province. Long before the revolution Henan's peasants learned to band together to fend off droughts and flooding of the Yellow River. Henan produced some of Mao's fiercest ideologues and communised faster than anywhere else. Mao called Henan his 'model province'. Today, Henan legally recognises Nanjie as a 'model village'.

We turn into the parking lot of a visitors' centre and for a small fee we get a battery-powered cart with fuzzy blue seats and a pony-tailed minder named Li Yan. 'Everything here is free,' she says in a hoarse, expressionless voice, 'including the food. There are 848 households and 3,000 resident members.' I listen politely as Lu Bo translates and explains a star system in which good work and a clean home are rewarded with points on a scale of one to ten, although some people manage to accumulate twelve. 'So instead of getting rich, they get points,' I say. Lu Bo smiles and agrees. It's as foreign to him as it is to me. Next we see where the residents live: fifteen buildings, six stories high. We pass factories (bricks, noodles, flour, spices), twenty-six ventures in all, and farmland where corn grows within city limits. 'Presumably if there's an invasion, they won't have to worry about food,' I say. Suddenly I feel feisty. I've barely seen a single person or vehicle on the street. 'Where is everybody?' I ask. Li Yan frowns as I start taking notes and suggests we take a break for lunch in Linying, since the free cafeterias in Nanjie have just closed. For the moment, I don't mind getting away. Nanjie looks like a Hollywood film set, empty of people and out of commission.

Exiting Nanjie through the city wall is like moving out of the time-melting emptiness of a Salvador Dalí painting and entering the sweat and sensuality of Hieronymus Bosch. Stench from rotting food and garbage mixes with aromas of steamy soups and oily dumplings as vendors fry and ladle food for noisy families. When I ask Mr Shao, the owner of the Happy Garden Restaurant, what he thinks of Nanjie, he's only too happy to wave his sword.

'He says it's full of losers who can't help themselves,' Lu Bo translates, and reels off the problems: bad management, outside competition, high bank debt and the inability to fire anyone. 'He also says Nanjie's corrupt and the GDP's been falling for three years, and to complicate matters the chief accountant recently dropped dead.' In a gesture of calm, Aaron pours a round of green tea but Lu Bo does nothing to soften the blows. 'When they opened the vault, huge piles of cash were discovered. Then, a few concubines arrived from the capital of Henan and even Beijing.' Concubine means 'little wife' in Chinese. Although they're officially illegal, it's not uncommon for men of means to keep them as mistresses throughout their lives. 'Each of the concubines brought a child and each one demanded money; so the party bosses paid them off in large and equal sums and told them never to return.'

Suddenly I feel guilty for hearing this; for stepping outside Nanjie's boundaries. Having travelled so far to experience the ideologically pure village, my escape into this rollicking, free to be bare-faced market town feels traitorous, unchaste.

*

The day before my visit to Nanjie, I went to the trendy Dashanzi art district on the outskirts of Beijing, popularly known as Factory 798. Designed by East Germans during the 1950s and paid for by the People's Republic of China, the industrial estate looks part-concentration camp, part-Bauhaus, with low, red brick buildings and oversized pipes running parallel to the maze of structures. Factory 798 is now an oasis for artists escaping the urban sprawl of fifteen million people.

An exhibit of photographs holds power. These are the same pictures I remember poring over in *Life Magazine* and *National Geographic* during the sixties and seventies, where smiling pig-tailed girls exactly my age held red books near their hearts and sang of their love for Red China, my country's enemy. How could these smiling children be my enemy? For decades, these were the only images of China available to the West. Here in the gallery, I learn that the person who took the pictures has a name – Xiao Zhung – and a philosophy. She was one of the few photographers who refused to stop working after the Communist victory in 1949, because she believed it was better to leave some kind of documentary record of the times, rather than no record at all.

Her photographs, all taken when she was employed by the Xinhua News Agency, are painstakingly composed. They show Red Guards frozen in dance steps as they celebrate the success of China's first nuclear missile launch in 1966; peasants performing the 'Loyalty Dance' with arms unnaturally arced upwards toward the face of Chairman Mao, radiating from the sun; cheering students and teachers gathered at a meeting called, 'Beating down anti-revolutionary ghosts'; grinning cotton weavers writing 'good news' letters about their annual quota to Mao; smiling families ignoring their rice bowls to read from their red books. As a child, the element of fantasy embedded in these photographs captivated me: model communes, model factories, model soldiers, and model children, living in smiling unison among hundreds of thousands of dressed-alike comrades in cities, towns and the countryside. A kind of ecstasy emanates from every picture, exporting a construction of happiness that the West was supposed to believe; that the Chinese people were supposed to believe; that the sensibilities of my childhood wished to believe. Now, two and a half decades into reform, Xiao Zhung calls her life's work by another name: 'The Irrational Times'.

*

I pretend to be in Red China during the seventies as we are led by Li Yan through Nanjie's instant, dried-noodle factory. Walking along the windows of a narrow corridor we observe an assembly line of girls down below, dressed in white. It looks like the Red China we talked about at my university on Sunday nights as we ate stir-fried tofu during gatherings of the US China People's Friendship Organisation, which I joined in part because I liked the food.

Now, years later, as I walk through the observation hall of a factory that made Nanjie wealthy and altered the eating habits of hundreds of millions of Chinese, I am somewhat wiser about the ideals and pitfalls of top-heavy political systems. For the moment, I focus on the fact that the assembly line looks paltry in an under-lit room the size of a gymnasium. Twenty girls stand behind a conveyor belt doing the *I Love Lucy* factory thing. Aaron points out that it takes three girls to fit one lid on each Styrofoam carton: one to slap it on, another to press it down and a third to re-seat it correctly. Although I know nothing about industrial efficiency, Aaron agrees that the shop floor is operating at ten or twenty per cent capacity. Li Yan sighs with exasperation, but by now I've given up asking her questions: such as why Nanjie looks under-populated; and why the factory of choice is under-performing; why we're not having a frank talk about the fact that Nanjie is in the doldrums. I don't see why we can't discuss the fact that no one (including profit-sharing Maoists) should have hard feelings that after dominating China's dried noodle market for nearly a decade, they suddenly face competition.

'Honestly,' I'd say to Li Yan, if we could have a proper girl-to-girl chat, 'it's nothing to be ashamed of. It can happen to anyone, really: depression, recession, corruption, scandal, whatever it is, you'll get over it, believe me. We all do.'

*

Before the itinerants were cleared out of my local underpass in Beijing this summer, it provided refuge from the heat for twenty or thirty Tibetan women and children whose homes are two and a half thousand miles away. Between naps, they fanned themselves on the ground beside their displays of beads, bangles, incense and plastic umbrellas. At both ends of the tunnel close to the stairs, their men crouched in circles, unflinchingly absorbed in cards and dice. Up above them, Nouveau Beijing is a city that's morphed into hyper commerce, fashion and consumerism; where the service and presentation of a meal at a themed restaurant can be mistaken for performance art, and brand names, real or fake, bring new ecstasies to shopping madness. Though the allure can be irresistible to the West, what often isn't reported are the number of disenfranchised, disturbed and disabled people to be found, from public parks and cavernous transport depots to little neighbourhood kiosks where they bundle up their belongings and sleep for the night. The number of wayfarers shoring up in Beijing is rising exponentially by the hundreds of thousands each year.

*

There is no need for moving vans in Nanjie. Every flat has identical furnishings; from the beds, sofas and open unit shelving to the red Mao clock that enshrines the main room. As Li Yan pulls up beside a tower block, she explains that two-bedroom flats go for two-generation families, three bedrooms for three generations and one, for a single generation on their own. We are going to meet Mr Duan, the Maoist party boss, who has arranged to introduce us to a family for Aaron to photograph; preferably three families of a peasant, worker and soldier, classic models of the revolution. Li Yan tells us that Mr Duan's model citizen has just moved into a three-generation flat because he has a new grandson. But when we go inside there is no sign of a baby; no sign of anyone, except for a taut man with a wolf-like face whose eyes fight back the tiniest kernel of interest in our meeting. His name is Sun Yan; he's sixty-five years old and has been cleaning toilets for forty years. Tension fills the air as we shake hands and take seats in the main room.

Aaron Deemer

Lu Bo begins: 'Mr Duan says a woman from California once brought him a T-shirt with Karl Marx on it. How would you like me to answer back?' Mr Duan gives me a wink; he's a pert man dressed in black from head to toe, apart from a white belt buckle with the word 'coyote' embossed in silver. I haven't brought a gift and I'm from Washington DC, so I think up something he might like – words and hope – and say it like I really mean it: 'The polem-ics of Marx and Mao should not be forgotten; Communism is to Capitalism as Yin is to Yang; In order to grasp the ideological under-pinnings of one system, you have to understand the other'. This does the trick and Mr Duan beams with approval.

'This is a woman with a passion for Communism!' he tells Lu Bo. Our hopes rise for Aaron's prospects of getting good pictures, but we have difficulty establishing where the other generations of Sun Yan's family are.

'His wife's away,' says Mr Duan.

'She's in the bedroom,' says Sun Yan, pointing toward a closed door. When pressed for the correct answer Mr Duan says that both sons are away. He doesn't mention the wife or what's behind the door but just to make sure we understand how hard the life of a toilet cleaner can be, Mr Duan tells us that Sun Yan couldn't get married until he was thirty-five years old.

'Who would want to marry someone with that job?' Mr Duan asks as Sun Yan hands me a stack of snapshots. Averting his eyes and nodding at all times when Mr Duan speaks, Sun Yan has the look of a man who's been through a bit of re-education. What I'd like to say to Mr Duan is, 'Would you kindly please leave so Sun Yan can open the door and Aaron can get on with his pictures?' Then I'd say to Sun Yan, 'So, how was the revolution? How'd you come to be a toilet cleaner all your life?' But instead I stick with the party line – how Maoism in Nanjie solved everybody's problems – and side-step man-made disasters in favour of a natural one.

'So how'd your family survive the famine of 1942?' I ask and Sun Yan promptly answers, 'We ate the bark of trees.'

I can't help thinking exactly what Mr Duan wants me to: If Sun Yan the toilet cleaner owes this spotless apartment and all his free provisions to Maoism, then bless Mao.

'The secret to Nanjie,' says Mr Duan, 'is the teachings of Chairman Mao. Maoist theory brings people without much education up.'

'But what exactly makes it *Maoist*?' I ask. 'What's the difference between, say, Nanjie and a kibbutz?' Lu Bo glares at me, repeating the sounds – kib-butz – and says he never heard this word. I restate the question substituting, 'classic communism minus Mao'. After some consultation, Lu Bo says that, 'Serve the People' is the core of Maoist theory. But confusion breaks out over a slogan that appears all over town: 'Only Fools Can Save China'.

'Surely you're translating wrong,' I say to Lu Bo. 'Surely Mr Duan is saying only *selfless* people can save China.' The party boss frowns at my suggestion so Lu Bo tries another tack with me.

'In Communist thinking, a man gives up everything, right?'

'Right.'

'He says, "Here, take my land, take my animals, take everything I own," right?'

'Right.'

'So the neighbours say, "He's a fool," right?'

'One might think.'

'Because only a fool would give up everything; so, only fools can save China.'

I nod slowly and Mr Duan nods too, locking eyes with me as he gives Lu Bo an earful: 'To serve the people is to work hard for society; Dedication is a worker who expects nothing in return; True and total dedication is a man who will put up with absolutely nothing in return.'

'I'm getting the gist,' I say.

'A suicide-bomber is an example of the total dedication Maoist theory means. Someone who throws himself in front of a tank is in keeping with core Maoist principles.' My nods stop but my eyes stay hooked on Mr Duan's. Who would have guessed that suicide bombing is a way of bringing Maoist theory up to date? Mr Duan has more news: Four other villages are turning Maoist, and seven thousand work units across China are now studying Maoist theory.

'Serve the People is what Maoist theory teaches!' Mr Duan says, raising his voice. 'You serve through discipline! You capitalists don't understand because you've never lived in a communist system!' Repeating the lessons of Mao – discipline, service and dedication as the staple of fools – Mr Duan jumps up and shakes our hands, a slight smile stealing his pinched expression when we realise we haven't taken any pictures.

*

When the time comes to catch our flight back to Beijing, our taxi driver, a Linying man, treats us to the same critique we've heard from Mr Shao, the restaurant owner, about the have-nots and hard-ups in Nanjie and their bosses' troubles: Corruption, Scandal, Concubines. But when asked to elaborate on local politics in Linying, the taxi driver's answer is no different: Corruption, Scandal, Concubines.

Thinking about Nanjie and the Maoist revolution on which it is based, I try and imagine my personality in a watch-and-listen but never-speak world, and how my record would be marred from birth: prone to mischief; driven only when on task; easily distracted by conflicting ideas. I assess my prospects for remaining in school during a Cultural Revolution-type era: Bleak. And my potential for leadership in the Red Guard: Grim. Recommendation for the coming years: Re-education in selflessness. The real question is whether or not I have what it takes to become a proper fool.

Travelling Alone

Anna Pollard

I had my first epileptic seizure when I was twelve years old. I found it traumatic. For many years I was seizure-free, but ten years ago that changed and I now have unpredictable attacks at least once every day. My neurologist has identified the site of abnormality in my brain and has tried, in vain, to control the force and frequency of my fits. As my seizures are tonic clonic, what used to be called *grand mal*, it is not safe for me to be alone. Without somebody to care for me during an attack I would take much longer to recover, physically, mentally and emotionally; I could injure myself; or die from asphyxiation. My epilepsy has not diminished my mental capabilities, determination or ambition but it has detrimentally affected my ability to fulfil my potential.

Reading has helped me accept my condition and the limitations it imposes upon me. It is one of the few activities that enable me to escape consciousness of the constant surveillance my disability demands. Reading *Silas Marner* by George Eliot in my teens was affirming as I identified with Silas, who has a form of epilepsy, and is portrayed as a loving man who is able to overcome adversity.

It is almost for Eliot as though catalepsy let mystery into the ordinary world or were a site of spiritual shake-up since both life-ruining and life-saving events occur while Silas is unaware in a fit. First a false friend, William Dane, steals money and blames it on Silas, causing him to be cast out of his close religious community, and to lose his fiancée. A watch had been set over the final hours of an elderly deacon. The man dies and the money goes missing while Silas is on duty and his own knife is beside the bureau where the money was kept:

> 'I must have slept,' said Silas. Then, after a pause, he
> added, 'Or I must have had another visitation like that
> which you have all seen me under, so that a thief must
> have come and gone while I was not in the body, but out
> of the body. But, I say again, search me and my dwelling,
> for I have been nowhere else.'

Lots are drawn to determine whether Silas is guilty, and Silas is confident that God will clear him, but the evidence against him convinces

the community that he must be lying. It is after he has been judged
that he realises William has framed him:

> 'You stole the money, and you have woven a plot to lay
> the sin at my door. But you may prosper, for all that: there
> is no just God that governs the earth righteously, but a
> God of lies, that bears witness against the innocent.'

In the opening six pages the reader has learnt all of this and more
and the stage is set for the drama of the novel. How will Silas react
when during another seizure a lost, friendless, golden-haired toddler
enters his life after her mother has died in the snow? Those of you
who have read the book know, and it would spoil it for the rest of
you if I were to tell.

The great Russian novelist Fyodor Dostoevsky was known to
have the condition. His work demonstrates his ability to overcome
the limitations that epilepsy imposed, and more importantly he used
his experience of the condition to create characters who are epileptic
in four of his twelve novels: Kirillov in *The Possessed*; Smirdyakov
in *The Brothers Karamazov*; Nellie in *The Insulted and Injured*; and
Prince Myshkin in *The Idiot*.

So far I have only read *The Idiot*. The main character, Prince
Myshkin, is represented positively but his vulnerability is evident
and the consequences of his condition are interrogated within the
body of text. He is considered to be the embodiment of Dostoevsky's
own views and his conception of the Christian ideal. The book
begins as he enters the world of the Russian ruling classes after a
four-year stay at a Swiss asylum. Myshkin is unable to integrate into
this society as his inherent goodness cannot be accommodated.
But Dostoevsky describes the character superbly in giving both the
outward and the inward manifestions of his condition. Outwardly
he is gentle and foolish, the idiot of the title:

> His eyes were large, blue and dreamy; there was some-
> thing gentle, though heavy-looking in their expression,
> something of that strange look from which some people
> can recognise at first glance a victim of epilepsy.

His inward experience is more violent. Dostoevsky shows what
happens in the mind and to the emotions of Prince Myshkin at the
onset of a seizure by giving a vivid description of the aura:

> He was thinking, incidentally, that there was a moment or
> two in his epileptic condition almost before the fit itself
> (if it occurred in waking hours) when suddenly amid

the sadness, spiritual darkness and depression, his brain seemed to catch fire at brief moments... His sensation of being alive and his awareness increased tenfold at those moments which flashed by like lighting. His mind and heart were flooded by a dazzling light. All his agitation, doubts and worries, seemed composed in a twinkling, culminating in a great calm, full of understanding... but these moments, these glimmerings were still but a premonition of that final second (never more than a second) with which the seizure itself began. That second was, of course, unbearable.

This description draws on Dostoevsky's own experiences, which becomes clear when reading the accounts he kept of his own seizures. *The Idiot* is challenging but it presents an authentic representation of life with frequent epileptic seizures.

The French novelist Gustave Flaubert was known to suffer from a nervous disorder which may have been epilepsy. In his novel *Flaubert's Parrot* the contemporary novelist Julian Barnes discusses epilepsy as he explores the nature of Flaubert's complaint. Epilepsy is not the main theme of the novel but Barnes uses aspects of the condition to enable him to better represent the psychological turmoil experienced by the main protagonist, Geoffrey Braithwaite. Towards the end of the text, in a section entitled *Braithwaite's Dictionary of Accepted Ideas*, the following quotation shows that a degree of resolution has been achieved by the main character:

EPILEPSY
Stratagem enabling Flaubert the writer to sidestep a conventional career, and Flaubert the man to sidestep life. The question is merely at what psychological level the tactic was evolved. Were his symptoms intense psychosomatic phenomena? It would be too banal if he merely had epilepsy.

The narrative form of this innovative text incorporates biography and literary criticism, making it highly informative. It is playfully written, often witty but never trite. It is also remarkably short, which is incredible, as it achieves so much.

The novels discussed above all directly relate to epilepsy. This is the exception rather than the rule in my reading. I enjoy reading novels on any subject, of any period, from any country and in any style. But, for me, the most wonderful aspect of the novel is the freedom it bestows upon me. Within its pages I can escape from my epilepsy and travel – alone – into innumerable fictional landscapes.

The Art of Wooing Nature

Susan Duncan

Eileen Pollard interviews Susan Duncan, consultant neurologist at the Neurosciences Centre in Greater Manchester with a special interest in epilepsy.

Can you remember learning to read?
Yes, I can. My mother was very enthusiastic that I should from an early age. She taught me my alphabet using a Scrabble set. She set the letters up on the racks and the game was that she'd start saying 'a' and then I would push the 'a' out. And then she would arrange these letters into little groups to make the words, but I have to say I didn't do it with great enthusiasm! My parents worked abroad and I think she'd started this because my schooling had been delayed and because we would soon be sailing to Africa to join my father. This was a way of keeping me entertained. And although I liked being told stories and I liked being read to, I wasn't too keen on learning to read myself. Then when I went to school at six it was really a question of what would be useful for my learning to write, because interestingly my mother hadn't taught me to write, she had only really taught me the letters. This was another trauma! The school I went to in Nigeria was run by Canadians and they had a rather synthetic way of going about it. That's when difficulties arose, because firstly their spelling is slightly different and secondly they didn't use phonics. And as a result my spelling is questionable; it's not that I'm dyslexic, but I only gradually began to get it together.

What was the first book I remember reading on my own? It's got to be one of Enid Blyton's. But I do remember that my father, to encourage me, started to read to me, and he read *Black Beauty*, which he had liked as a boy, and I thought it was wonderful. My father's favourite author was Robert Louis Stevenson – and of course coming from Edinburgh that provided a link with Stevenson – so he got out *Treasure Island*. I suspect my father is still traumatised by this to this day. *Treasure Island* was going very well, and if you've read Stevenson you'll know he's a very vivid writer. We got to the scene with Blind Pew coming to the inn to tip the black spot to Billy Bones, the old drunkard sitting in the bar. To this day I can remember the tap, tap, tapping of the stick and the green shade covering his eyes; and especially his grip on the boy Jim Hawkins and saying 'Take me in to the captain' and giving him the black spot. This was intensely vivid and I thought extremely frightening – so frightening I refused to let my father read any further. In fact I would have nothing more to do with the book, it had to be put away. And that rather cured me, until I was an adult, of Robert Louis Stevenson and also of anything which I perceived to be frightening.

Looking back, would you say that there were any books that were crucial in your developing career?
As a doctor, as a medical student, one book that stays with me, which I came across quite by chance, is *Awakenings* by Oliver Sacks. This was his first book and two things struck me about it. The first was that it was dedicated to W. H. Auden. In fact Auden had written a little piece at the front saying 'I've read *Awakenings* and I think it's a masterpiece'. And then there's this quotation from Auden, whose father was a doctor: 'Pa used to say that medicine is the intuitive art of wooing nature'. I thought that was fascinating. I was either a first- or second-year medical student. *Awakenings* is basically a medical casebook of descriptive neurology, describing these unfortunate people who'd had what we'd call 'sleeping sickness' – it was part of the 'flu pandemic in 1919. Some of these people, a few years down the line or in some cases quite shortly after the initial infection, went on to develop very severe forms of something like Parkinson's disease. Some of these were looked after by their families but most had made their way into institutions; the book makes it clear that many of these people had been highly intelligent and they remained so, and when they *could* communicate they communicated very well. In the late 1960s, they were given L-DOPA [levodopa], which had been introduced to treat Parkinson's disease, and it was reasoned that it should also be tried on this group.

What was fascinating in Sacks' account wasn't *purely* medical; it was the *relationship* these people had with their condition – the accommodations they had made to live their lives with this condition, and the accommodations that their families had made, and indeed the way that elements of the condition were subsumed into their personality and became part of them. And then L-DOPA came on the scene. They were liberated, *awakened* from their condition but then, after a period of time, they began to experience some of the side-effects of L-DOPA, which in those days were very dramatic because they used such high doses. Even so, it's intriguing to me that a few of the patients decided, having had a wonderful year on this drug, that actually they would prefer to be back the way they had been before. Somehow they had grown to accommodate what they were. I have carried *Awakenings* with me throughout my medical career.

I think that now that students are studying this area and models of health are being taught there is a stronger *social* idea of illness, which we didn't learn about when I was a student because it was a predominantly biological approach then. I was talking to a GP recently who said 'Our idea of what's good health is often completely at odds with what our punters think! They come in with this idea that they're not well and even if they are, they have decided that something's not working for them, something's not right for them and they wish it put right, even if we can't do so.' Health is not an absolute but is individual to us all.

Oliver Sacks uses this term 'a dis-ease with the world', and I think much of what we see in neurology is exactly that; in fact, I'd say a quarter of the new patients I see are exhibiting a 'dis-ease' with the world. They're working too hard, their working environments are harsh, they're not getting on with their families, they have disappointments in life, and this manifests itself in low-level periods of tingling, palpitations of the heart etc., which are interpreted as signs of something else.

What was it that you responded to in Sacks' book – was it that mixture of the personal and the medical?
Yes and I think *Awakenings* is still his best book because he gave a lot of thought to the interface between the emotional aspects and the psychological aspects of what was being called a 'chronic neurological condition', and how people accommodate these aspects by subsuming them into part of their being – it's quite Freudian.

The other book by Sacks which I really enjoyed was *Seeing Voices*. It's set in an American college, the only college in America for people who are deaf. And again it comes down to our perceptions of people who are different. They are all people who are profoundly deaf but who sign, and the first question is, should these people be *made* to talk? Most of the students were determined that they should sign because this is part of their deaf inheritance and their community. The staff of the college at that time were nearly all hearing, though some of them could sign, and the book recounts the changes that went on and how the students felt very strongly that the staff of the college should sign, and preferably, be deaf too. It also explored how people communicate with their hands and illustrated that the subtleties and nuances that we bring with our voices they could bring with their signing. The other thing I learnt, which is fascinating, is that British Sign Language [BSL] is different from American Sign Language [ASL]. Whereas America speaks English, or a version of it, ASL has more links to French, because it was a Frenchman who pioneered signing there. Each country seems to have its own version of sign language. ASL is based on one-hand signing whilst BSL is based on two-hand signing. The book made very interesting points about how we communicate and the subtleties of it. Plus, it proved that people who have chronic conditions form communities; some people see their condition as intrinsic to themselves while others don't. Sacks didn't touch on it in his book but there are of course people who step out of the deaf community because they get cochlear implants, and interestingly those people do attract a lot of reproach from some areas of the deaf community. People build themselves into communities around medical facts.

I watched a programme about a school where they taught deaf children to speak. They used balloons and the children picked up the sounds through the balloon. They interviewed several of the ex-pupils and it was really heartbreaking. This young man said that he couldn't be a part of the deaf community – he felt that that had been taken away from him before he could even make a decision, because he was so young when he learned to speak. And then he said 'And of course I probably don't even sound the same as a hearing person'. These were two massive things that he was never going to get over. You see these communities forming with people with epilepsy too. These days we have – for some people – the opportunity to do surgery and stop the seizures and it's very interesting that there are some who never quite adjust to being 'cured'. They seem to themselves to have lost part of their own character. It's quite an interesting transition; people discover that, yes, they are expected to learn to drive and to get out and get a job and replace a life that they've never had before. Now some want that; they have moved from one community to another, and for them it's a relatively smooth transition. You get others who are not happy that their life is shifting. We had a very successful patient who then developed pain from their operation scar, and this became the entire focus of this individual's life; it's fascinating how after one chronic promblem was cured, another surfaced.

It is about communities: you've got epilepsy, you go to a support group, your entire life revolves around this disease, it's part of *you*;

and then if you cease to have that illness, part of your identity goes. You have to be able to step into another world, and the people who do it well are generally the ones who really want a cure. Some people don't make that transition and some people choose not to.

People's relationships with their epilepsy can be quite intimate because it is so much a part of them. It seems to depend on how they interpret their seizures: some people interpret them as a connection with another world, a different dimension, and consequently if they lose that, they feel that they've lost a portal into another field. When my epilepsy was active and I came out of a seizure there was a kind of altered perception, it seemed that the fabric of time was stretching. And there was that feeling of hovering between two dimensions. I don't get that now. So I can understand why some people feel that epilepsy is an intimate part of them, a facet of them – rather like musical ability.

My mum said to me quite recently 'I know that when I come out of seizures sometimes I can be a bit slow, and I know that's very hard for you all, but it's still me, it's still part of me'. Personally I find that quite distressing because to me, that's not mum, not at all, but I can see that to her – who *else* is it going to be, if it's not her?

I think for some people they want to have control, and with epilepsy there is the feeling that people will take control of you, they perceive that you're disabled, so they start making decisions or doing things for you that you may not be happy with. The aspect of losing control I think is as frightening and as disadvantageous to you as the experiential aspects of having a seizure, the déjà vu and so on.

There are many disadvantages.

Auden's father is so perceptive with that comment about the intuitive art of wooing nature. The individual is always in the picture.

Here's a challenge – can you recommend a list of books or writers you have enjoyed?

Robert Louis Stevenson for his vividness; Graham Greene for his characterisation, Jane Austen for her quick delineation of character and situation. They're the writers I keep coming back to. But in selecting individual titles I'd go for the different but equally sustained structures of *To Kill a Mockingbird* by Harper Lee and *The Good Soldier* by Ford Madox Ford, and Philip Roth's *American Pastoral* as a lengthy yet cleverly structured novel.

Thank you for talking to *The Reader*.

Three Poems by Richard Livermore

The Go-Between

In case you should ever
wonder or ask
what remains
of the messenger's task,

it is to engender
faith in the dark,
faith like the eyeless
faith of the quark

responding to other
quarks in the fire
and forging a cosmos
out of desire.

The Heron-God

The angle-poise heron darts
a spear into the river, parts
the water as did God the sea
for Moses and the Jews to flee.

And for all the fish can tell,
the heron is a god as well,
who parts the water from the sky
and singles out which fish should die.

My Current Account

The number of years
I currently owe
compared to forty
or fifty ago,

is minus the forty
or fifty foresaid
to be that number
less in the red.

But who can foresay
how many I lack
before I am finally
all in the black.

Researching Reading Groups

Suzanne Hodge

How do you go about researching reading groups? And what effect does being in one have on your health and well-being? These are the questions I have been grappling with over the last few months as I have been working with the Get into Reading project to explore the health and social benefits of community reading groups. The Get into Reading (GiR) project is run by The Reader, in partnership with Birkenhead and Wallasey Primary Care Trust and Job Centre Plus, and with funding from the Paul Hamlyn Foundation. It aims to promote reading as an activity that can bring a range of benefits, from improving people's literacy skills and increasing their confidence to helping them cope with the stresses of everyday life. The project runs fifteen reading groups that meet in libraries and community centres across the Wirral, an area in which there are extremes of affluence and deprivation in close proximity to each other.

Having obtained a small amount of funding to do a pilot study I have spent the last few months getting to know more about the groups and how they work. I went to six of the fifteen groups, sitting in on meetings and observing what goes on. One of the groups agreed to be a case study for me, so I attended all of their meetings over several weeks, and talked to members about what led them to join the group and what they get out of it.

You might ask what makes *these* reading groups different to the thousands of others that meet up and down the land. Like most reading groups, they provide a relaxed and sociable setting in which their members can read books and then enjoy discussing them with others. The range of books that GiR groups read is perhaps wider than that of most reading groups, taking in Shakespeare and the great nineteenth-century novels as well as modern fiction. What makes these reading groups special though is that they have drawn in people who might never have found their way to a regular book club. This is partly because they have been set up specifically with certain marginalised sections of society in mind, such as carers, mothers of young children, people with mental health problems, users of a drug rehabilitation service and residents of a YMCA. But it is also due to the unusual way the groups work. First of all they are led by trained and skilled facilitators who give gentle guidance, encouraging members to think about what they have read and how it relates to their own lives. And unlike most reading groups which meet monthly, GiR reading groups meet every week. This means there is a much greater degree of continuity, both social and literary. But what is most distinctive about the groups is that whilst in most reading groups members read at home and meet primarily to discuss the book, the GiR groups actually do most of the reading out loud in their meetings. This is seen both by the facilitators and by the group members as an essential element of the groups' success. As one reading group member explained it to me:

> I don't think there's anything nicer than sitting there listening to somebody reading to you, I find that really relaxing. It's as though you can just let your mind wander and you get all your imaginary pictures of how certain characters are, I think that enhances it. It's as though, I don't know, a different part of your brain is involved again. It gets you thinking a bit more because you're listening.

Another member described it as 'a form of therapy'. Attending the groups as an academic observer I found this aspect of the groups both fascinating and also challenging to my own academic 'objectivity'. I was there to observe people's interaction and to understand the dynamic of the groups, but there were times when it was impossible not to be drawn in completely, to become part of the phenomenon I was observing. Listening to the poetry and stories, I experienced my own moments of personal illumination, made all the more powerful because those moments were being shared with people who had been complete strangers to me before I entered the room.

The case study group that I attended was particularly sociable and welcoming to new members, including myself, and I enjoyed re-reading *Wuthering Heights* with them, a book I had not picked up since studying it as an A-level set text. Over the weeks, it was interesting to see how the group responded to the book. At the outset, I feared that they might not get any further than the first chapter as someone would interrupt every time they came across a word that was unfamiliar, asking the facilitators for definitions. And then as different characters were introduced into the plot there was confusion over who was related to whom. However, by the end of the first chapter the interruptions ceased as everyone started to be drawn into the story. Talking to people individually it was interesting to hear the different reactions to the book, some people loving it immediately, others finding it difficult at first but coming round to liking it, as one young woman explained:

I'm starting to enjoy it more now it's coming to the end but to begin with I wasn't. It was quite hard to get into because it's not a book I'd ever think of picking up. It has been nice the way that you're reading something completely different.

There are about eight regular members of this group, ranging from their 20s to their 80s. The group was set up with mothers of young children in mind, so they have free use of a crèche in the community centre next to the library where they meet. About half of the members are young mothers and talking to them it was clear that the group gives them something valuable. It provides them with an hour-and-a-half each week when they can relax in good company and enjoy reading or being read to, knowing that their children are being taken care of nearby. Without the structure of the group some of them would find reading at home impossible. One young woman explained that when they were set a chapter of *Wuthering Heights* to read at home before the next session she read it out loud to her 10-month-old twins after feeding them. Not only did this enable her to fit the reading into her daily routine, but she was pleased to find that the children seemed to enjoy being read to, even though the reading matter might normally have been considered to be a little beyond them!

Then there are the older members of the group, a widower who comes along with his daughter and an elderly lady who also lives alone and was persuaded to join the group by the librarians who run it and who were concerned that she seemed isolated and depressed. Both these individuals were already active readers, so for them coming to the group has been mainly about finding social support and companionship, although it has also expanded their literary horizons beyond their regular diet of books by local authors and war fiction.

In academic terms my time spent with the GiR groups has been valuable in helping me, with colleagues, to develop an extensive research study that will assess the health and social worth of community reading groups in a more systematic and in-depth way. From initial observations it seems that the benefits are many and varied. The groups help to make books accessible and enjoyable, encouraging people who read little to read more and introducing people to books they might never have attempted. They help to increase literacy skills and confidence, and they provide a source of social support and companionship for those who might otherwise live isolated lives. But I have also gained on a human level from my encounters with the reading groups. The lasting impressions that I have of the groups are ones of warmth and of the real pleasure that reading as a shared experience can bring.

Readers Connect

In partnership with Oxford World's Classics

Welcome to **Readers Connect**, a new feature which aims to promote the pleasure of reading in groups, and to offer readers encouragement to engage with the classics. In the current popular tide of reading groups, such a mission has never been more apt, nor more crucial. There is something for all readers. If you are already a member of a reading group or thinking of joining one, **Readers Connect** will be a source of new ideas and of lively debate; while for unaffiliated or solitary readers we hope **Readers Connect** will become the most flexible and accessible form of reading group.

There are three ways to take part:

Connect with a Classic: There are many readily available booklists for reading groups, but nearly all of them offer modern bestsellers. We want reading groups to have a go at some of the neglected classic fiction that has so much to offer in romance, suspense, thrills and thoughtfulness. In each issue you will find a range of essays, giving general introductions and close readings of one chosen classic novel. There will be competitions to win copies of the novel, courtesy of Oxford World's Classics, for your reading group. We start with Edith Wharton's *The House of Mirth*.

Starting Short: Reading groups don't have to be prearranged; they don't have to happen once a month in a library or a bookshop. Here is an alternative. A short story will be available to download for free on The Reader website: www.thereader.co.uk. Print off as many copies as you like and hand them out to your family, friends or workmates. Read out loud to your husband or wife before going to bed. Discuss the story over a meal, during a coffee break or on the way to work. If you're not sure where to start, have a look at the suggestions and ideas offered online by the Reader staff. Email your thoughts, ideas, difficulties, pleasures and pains to readers@liv.ac.uk

Meet the Reading Group: Write in and give other readers a glimpse into the secret world of your group! In each issue members of a reading group describe their group and recommend titles to try.

There will be discounts on the featured books from Oxford World's Classics, and special subscription deals for reading groups.

Connect with a Classic
Edith Wharton, *The House of Mirth*

Mourning in
The House of Mirth

Jane Davis

The heart of the wise is in the house of mourning; but the
heart of fools is in the house of mirth.

Ecclesiastes

One of Edith Wharton's best works, *The House of Mirth* is sometimes called 'a novel of manners' but there is nothing gentle
here. The world the book describes (upper-class New York circa
1900) is a Darwinian arena where creatures must fight tooth and
claw for survival, and for the reader the experience of the book
is like being caught in a remorseless and excruciating trap, being
crushed and squeezed until one longs for, and yet still dreads, the
end. It's too long to read at a sitting but I found myself keeping it in
my bag and reading it in shop queues or at red lights.

The novel opens with an accidental meeting one hot afternoon,
between the beautiful unmarried twenty-nine-year-old Lily Bart,
and Lawrence Selden, a not-very-wealthy bachelor a little older than
her: 'Selden paused in surprise. In the afternoon rush of the Grand
Central Station his eyes had been refreshed by the sight of Miss
Lily Bart.' Edith Wharton is mistress of the telling word and here
'refreshed' is the two-edged sword. Lily *is* lovely on the eye amid the
mad bustle of the rush-hour station; she *is* a refreshing sight. And
refreshment has a place in the world: tea, art, house parties, European
travel, and flirtatious conversation are all delightful restoratives. But
how does refreshment stack up against steely social convention or
the power commanded by Wall Street? If Lily can't be more than a
sort of refreshment the world will pick her up and put her down as
lightly as a cup of tea. As indeed it may be about to do:

> Selden had never seen her more radiant. Her vivid head,
> relieved against the dull tints of the crowd, made her

more conspicuous than in a ball-room, and under her
dark hat and veil she regained the girlish smoothness, the
purity of tint that she was beginning to lose after eleven
years of late hours and indefatigable dancing.

'Indefatigable' carries the whispered suggestion that Lily Bart
couldn't stop dancing if she wanted to, that there is something
almost machine-like, something of the humanised automaton, about
her. And there's an ominous note in the only momentary reversal of
time: 'she *regained* the girlish smoothness' that really 'she was *beginning* to lose'. Soon she will be too old to be marriageable. And yet
these insinuating thoughts have hardly time to percolate through
the reader's consciousness before the next paragraph comes. Lily
begs for help, Selden offers tea, and away they go:

> He led her through the throng of returning holidaymakers,
> past sallow-faced girls in preposterous hats, and flat-chested
> women struggling with paper bundles and palm-leaf fans.
> Was it possible she belonged to the same race? The din-
> giness, the crudity of this average section of womanhood
> made him feel how highly specialised she was.

'Highly specialised' is the Darwinian phrase that pins Lily momentarily to the dissecting table, forcing us to acknowledge that she is
performing a function in a social eco-system and that this offers
both a means of survival and a restriction of personal human
freedom. The survival-function restricts as powerfully as any external material constraint: the beautiful woman who must marry well
is as trapped as any of the 'sallow-faced girls in preposterous hats,
and flat-chested women struggling with paper bundles'. The novel is
about the deepest constraints, social, biological, personal.

But Lily is never *simply* conventional. Here at the opening of
the novel she flouts the rules by getting Selden to offer her tea –
they'll be alone together – in his apartment:

> They both laughed, and he knelt by the table to light the
> lamp under the kettle, while she measured out the tea
> into a little teapot of green glaze. As he watched her hand,
> polished as a bit of old ivory, with its slender pink nails,
> and the sapphire bracelet slipping over her wrist, he was
> struck with the irony of suggesting to her such a life as
> his cousin Gertrude Farish had chosen. She was so evi-
> dently the victim of the civilisation which had produced
> her, that the links of her bracelet seemed like manacles
> chaining her to her fate.

They may laugh at the poverty of Gertie Farish's (spinsterly, flat-dwelling) life but it is nonetheless (see that key word) a 'chosen' life, self-authenticating. Meanwhile Lily is trapped in the house of mirth and must be gay: the sapphire bracelet is, as Selden observes, 'chaining her to her fate'. And yes, it may be that Lily is 'the victim of the civilisation which had produced her' but the power of this novel is its remorseless investigation into Lily's own choice to continue to wear that bracelet until it cuts away her flesh. Terrifying. And true. *The House of Mirth*, just over a hundred years old, has many contemporary resonances. I finished it wondering why no one can write such a novel now, about our world. Are all our writers wearing those bracelets?

That Latent Sense

Terence Davies

Frances Macmillan talks to director Terence Davies about his film adaptation of Edith Wharton's The House of Mirth

What was the first book you read and loved?
Jane Eyre was my first great book, which I read at fourteen or fifteen. But before that I remember reading the Famous Five books and loving them: we had a full set of them at my primary school, and I tried to read them all. They were so romantic: they were always set in places like Cornwall, and there were always smuggler rings... It was terribly adventurous when you live in an urban slum.

Do you remember which books were lying around your house when you were growing up?
There were none. Books were all read at school. We had a little lean-to in the yard, and a very old sideboard had been put in there. Once when I was fourteen or so, I opened the sideboard drawer and found two novels: *The Hunchback of Notre Dame* and *Jane Eyre*. My oldest brother said '*Jane Eyre*, that's a good book'. I don't know how he knew; my family tended not to be readers, at least not at home. But I read *Jane Eyre* and loved it. When I left school at fifteen I spent the whole of the next year reading; I read the whole of Dickens, and read all the Brontës – I just read for a year.

Do you still read constantly nowadays, is the same appetite there?
No, I have to say. I don't read any modern fiction because when I try I can't get past the first few chapters, it strikes me as being so lifeless. And the other thing, you go into a bookshop and everything is 'a masterpiece', 'a stunning debut' – but they can't all be! Once there was joy in going into a bookshop and buying things you didn't know, but now… I'm not going to buy a book to struggle through one or two chapters and then put it down.

What about poetry?
It's my great love. I remember the first poem I ever read was 'The Highwayman' by Alfred Noyes and I know every verse even now – I learnt that when I was thirteen. I love Betjeman because he makes me laugh and he's a wonderful poet too. Poems like 'A Subaltern's Love Song' or 'The Hunter Trials' are truly funny. I memorise them, and run them through my mind again and again, and it gives me enormous pleasure.

When I was sixteen or seventeen we got our first television, and over four nights Alec Guinness read the entire *Four Quartets* by T. S. Eliot from memory, which was absolutely knockout. They became my mantra; I still read them at least once a month. I think they are the greatest achievement in poetry in the twentieth century. I like Larkin very much, and Emily Dickinson – I'm now discovering poems of hers I haven't read, like 'If You Were Coming In The Fall', which is just heartbreakingly wonderful. And I couldn't live without the sonnets of Shakespeare.

Are there novels that you return to in the same way?
Not in the same way. I still love *Jane Eyre*. It's not a perfect novel by any means, but it's written in such white heat, there are parts of it which still make me cry and move me so deeply, like the end of Chapter 4, before she's sent to Lowood – it's heartbreaking – 'Even for me life had its gleams of sunshine'. But my favourite novel is *Bleak House*. I saw it many, many years ago on television. They did it on a Friday night on BBC1, really cheaply, with shaking scenery! But there was an old actress called Nora Nicholson, who was the most wonderful Miss Flyte. Then I went and bought it. And that opening was fabulous: from way, way out in long shot you're getting slowly closer and closer to London, then closer, closer into Chancery Lane, with that wonderful metaphor of fog. It's one of the great, great opening chapters in all literature.

When you read something, does it always play like a film inside your head?

It's hard to say. *Bleak House* is immensely cinematic. The opening of *Jane Eyre* is immensely cinematic: the rain and the cold, and her great feeling of being inferior. But with a great novel, you see it visually, or at least I do, and I assume everyone sees it visually. As soon as I read the opening of *The House of Mirth* I knew what the shots were. With a novel I didn't like, I wouldn't know where to put the camera. It's in the text and it's what you see when you read the text. It's an instinctive thing.

Let's talk about *The House of Mirth*...
When I came to do the adaptation, there were certain things I felt I had to change. For instance, I conflated the characters of Gertie Farish and Grace Stepney. Separate, they're not that interesting, but if you amalgamate them, taking Gertie's unrequited love for Lawrence Selden and putting it into Grace, then the latter's nastiness is all the more powerful: while it's apparently Christian rectitude in fact it's sexual jealousy – she sees that Lawrence loves Lily.

You can do that in film: there are areas which you can make more subtle, just as there are times when you have to use broader strokes. For example, Aunt Julia has to be made more fearsome. In the book, she's not a very intelligent woman, and is cruel because of that lack of intelligence. But in the film you have to make her stronger and grimmer, because she's only in it for a short time. In that sense the characterisation for Aunt Julia is relatively crude. Eleanor Bron, who played Aunt Julia in the film and plays her marvellously I think, told me she'd just finished reading the book and that she completely disagreed with how I'd written Aunt Julia. In fact, that made her performance all the greater because she was able then to give me exactly what I wanted.

Gertie provides Lily with some sort of refuge or solace; I wondered if you removed her in order to turn out a light for Lily.
Not really, no. I don't think Lily has any choices. Because it is a tragedy, her trajectory is fixed. At the beginning, she's rather superficial and not that attractive as a person. Because if you're beautiful, if you've had a comfortable life and you expect to marry well, then why should you think about morality? It's only when Lily starts her downward decline that huge questions of personal morality and integrity come to the fore. She can't do what the others do, which is to have their peccadilloes on the side without getting caught. Lily thinks she knows how to play this game, but she has no idea. She thinks, in the case of her friend's rich husband, Gus Trenor, 'If I charm him, he will help me, and that will be enough.' But of course it's not enough; it's a

complete misreading of the situation. He expects sexual favours, and assumes that she knows that. When Lily is in fact morally shocked by the idea, of course Gus thinks she's hypocritical. Lily fulfils what she says in the film (but not in the book), 'My genius would appear to be to do the right thing at the wrong time'. Or vice versa.

Where do you think Lily's moral compass comes from? Does it grow in her or is it always there?
Very often we don't know our own motives or why we do things. We simply don't. But *something* prevents us from certain actions. Some people have no problem with, say, being sexually predatory; others have. Although Lily doesn't know it at the beginning, she does have that latent sense of morality. When she gets to the point when she could shut out that latent sense, when she has the chance to marry Percy Gryce for his millions, she can't do it. She doesn't realise anything consciously, it's an instinct.

Which brings us to another decision you made in the film adaptation: Lily is in possession of love letters which her enemy Bertha Dorset had sent to Lawrence Selden, with which she could blackmail Bertha and thus win back her lost position in society. Near the end of the novel, Lily sets off to the Dorsets with the letters, but then she passes Lawrence's door and decides, instinctively, to go to him instead. In the film, you make her go a little further, all the way to the Dorsets' house. But the Dorsets are not at home.
No, that's not in the book. We've come back to doing the right thing at the wrong time, or vice versa. When in the film Lily finally decides to use the letters, the Dorsets are away, they've gone to the country. All the life goes out of her then – there's nothing to do but go to see Lawrence and destroy the letters. That's putting a little extra something into the tragedy – what if she'd gone two days earlier? Would she have been able to blackmail Bertha? I doubt it. Bertha would have turned the situation around and pulled Lily to pieces. Bertha is an anaconda! Lily is a rabbit.

So it was a decision to heighten the sense of tragic chance? In the book, it seems barely an actual intention.
In the film (once again, this isn't in the book), Rosedale says to Lily, 'Why don't you use the letters? It would be so easy. It is so easy'. But it's not. If you are not by nature a blackmailer and a dissembler, you can't do something like that.

Lily wants Lawrence to know that she has 'saved herself whole from the seeming ruin of her life'. Is there any redemption in that wholeness for Lily at the end of the book or is it utterly tragic?

I think it is a kind of redemption, but at a huge cost. It makes you wonder about moral integrity – is it worth it? But if you are a moral person, then it is worth it.

You said that the opening scenes of *The House of Mirth* immediately appeared in your head you were reading it, but it strikes me as such an interior world – much of the action occurs inside people's heads. I wondered why your response to such an interior world was to make it visual. What was it you wanted people to see in particular?
It's not a conscious thing. It's instinctive. You know what the story must be and content dictates form, never the other way around. The book's sub-textual meaning tells you how to shoot the film. But of course there are difficulties, as with the character of Mrs Hatch who has no dialogue at all – instead you are told about her in just one page – so you have to put in dialogue and make it sound like Edith Wharton. Or again at the Van Osburgh wedding, we had to tell the audience in a succinct way that they are watching a wedding. What do all weddings have in common? Photographs. The photographer would see the image upside down. So you have the image upside down, 'I now pronounce you man and wife', and *pouf!* they're the right way up. A wedding. In the book you can go easily from 'Part One' to 'Part Two' but that wouldn't work in a film. You've got to get the sub-textual meaning across. So I played the *Così fan tutte* duet, which is all about hope, love, love returning. We see New York at the end of the season; it's raining, the camera is travelling across water and then the water is dappled with sunlight because we've moved to the Mediterranean. This might not be in the book, but it's a cinematic way of conveying a change of scene and with it Lily's hope that she will go on a cruise with the Dorsets and meet a rich husband.

How would you recommend *The House of Mirth* to individuals or groups who normally steer clear of the classics, who prefer modern books?
To start with, the writing is sensational. It's a fabulous story, a genuine tragedy, but in a way, it's a thriller, a moral thriller. It's about the cruelty of a society which has these elaborate rules, and you don't know exactly what they are, but if you break them retribution is lethal and swift. That's a thriller! And it's fabulous English; she's better than Henry James, I think. You should take the time to read it, and interpret it for yourself.

Thank you for your wonderful work, and for giving your time to *The Reader.*

Location, Location, Location

Our Spy visits Edith Wharton's New York

Enid Stubin

I first read *The House of Mirth* almost twenty-five years ago, when it appeared on my doctoral comprehensives list and, along with two dozen masterworks of American Literature, had to be consumed on a tight schedule. Sitting at a grungy table in Bobst Library, a Philip Johnson-designed joke, I devoured the book in a day and then moped around in a haze of grief for the sacrificial Lily Bart and the gilt chain of miscalculation leading to her fall.

Asked to revisit the novel for *The Reader*, I outfitted myself with a cheap paperback edition, assiduously avoided the introduction by Anna Quindlen, which I knew would irritate me, and read it on subway commutes to Brooklyn, on bus rides to the Upper West Side and in a doctor's waiting room on Park Avenue, around the corner from the Morgan Museum, with its fabled library belonging to the industrialist – that is, I carried Wharton's book through a New York City replete with the evidence of ambition and class attainment and anxieties, along streets teeming with spellbound tourists, doughty stroller-pushing moms, elegant matrons, and the tense young professionals of the new middle class. And I had to marvel at the mere century of change in New York, seemingly the most fluid of playgrounds for all sorts of acts of social subversion, where marriage to money still confers status (the Ron Perelman–Ellen Barkin ménage was written up rosily in *The New Yorker* just before it fell apart at the seams) while divorce makes for a pleasingly communal *schadenfreude*. In this context, Wharton's accomplishment dazzles us, not only in the creation of a heroine as flawed and compelling as Lily, but in the geography of a city inimical to human aspiration.

Critics have mentioned the social claustrophobia of the novel, the insularity of important families who look very much like those of Wharton's own milieu. But the hothousy habitat of the Trenors, Van Osburghs, and Dorsets is circumscribed by the very topography of New York; 'the country' and Monte Carlo seem mere cardboard backdrops for the leisure-time activities of the dim and wealthy. Fifth Avenue is established as the socio-economic locus of affluence and power and also serves as a *cordon sanitaire*, bifurcating the city and zoning the haves from the have-nots. The novel is hemmed in, both socially and spatially. Once family and friends close ranks against Lily, Fifth Avenue, no longer a vector toward fulfillment and acceptance, becomes a cul de sac.

At the very beginning of the novel, Lily confesses her 'luxury of discontent' as she settles into an armchair in Selden's flat off Madison Avenue for tea and a frank discussion of her limitations and requirements, her very presence there an indiscretion that delights them both for a moment before the world has its say: '...you know I am horribly poor – and very expensive. I must have a great deal of money'. The next day, having decamped to Bellomont, the Trenors' country estate, where she begins a campaign to ensnare a wealthy dolt, Lily gauges her happiness by the spaciousness of the guest room through whose windows she sees 'a perspective of lessening formality to the free undulations of the park'. But this is no Penshurst; there are no natural correspondences between luxury and merit, and the price of Judy Trenor's hospitality includes the loss of three hundred dollars in a single night's game of bridge and the undreamt-of and unwelcome presumption of Gus Trenor. A brilliant marriage, which seems less and less important to her emotionally, as her musings demonstrate, is actually Lily's only way out.

Marriage comes in for a drubbing; instead of a guarantor of ease and content, it is seen as 'retaliation', a satisfying way for women and men to get even with each other and their former detractors. The once-rakish Jack Stepney, now 'thickened and grown prudish', marinates in boredom with the woman he courted for her money. The 'little Jew' Rosedale has on-and-off plans for Lily, just as she plots to settle scores by affiancing herself to him: 'As the wife of Rosedale – the Rosedale she felt it in her power to create – she would at least present an invulnerable front to the enemy'.

In the subtlety of her characterization, Wharton limns Lily's perverse need to wreck her own designs, following impulse instead of obeying the requirements of her strategy. Whether this is born of appetite or caprice is unclear, and Wharton puts the canny evaluation of this dynamic in the mouth of Carry Fisher: 'That's Lily all over, you know: she works like a slave preparing the ground and sowing her seeds, but the day she ought to be reaping the harvest, she oversleeps herself or goes off on a picnic'. Through Carry's confidences to Selden we learn that the matter of the Italian prince involved the inopportune appearance of 'a good-looking stepson'. None of this is anything we know from Lily; rather it is said about her, and not only because she elicits fascinated gossip but because even in this insular world, others read her better than she does herself. Only in the bruised, luminous exchanges with Selden does any consciousness or self-knowledge appear, and this is revealed dramatically rather than internalized. Their intimate conversation alerts us to a Lily we have not seen heretofore. What emerges from her lips is genuinely astounding, unlike the stilted dialogue of her alternately halting and imperious dealings with the working classes.

Eventually brought to serve as a cultural adviser to Mrs. Norma Hatch and moving to the Emporium Hotel, Lily notes the 'vague metropolitan distances' covered in carriage or motor car by the fashionable demimondaines. In contrast, Gerty Farish chafes at the cramped apartment where a distraught Lily once came for comfort after the debacle with Gus Trenor. Selden will also observe, as he paces in Gerty's drawing room, the 'circumscribed space' in which a poor and unhandsome woman is consigned to live, just as earlier he brooded over the motto engraved on Lily's stationery, 'Beyond!', which he registers as 'a cry for rescue'.

Lily's stunning success at tableaux vivants echoes the scene in Vanity Fair but with a tragic resonance: Becky Sharp is delighted by her success but shrewdly aware that it is only a rung on the social ladder she means to ascend. The more naïve Lily is mesmerized by the response to her beauty and her superior style, and she sees her reception as good enough reason to put off Selden. It's not clear what she thinks the admiration of the evening will bring her. Throughout the novel, she's a bit confused and confusing: Wharton has not provided her or the reader with a clear analysis of Lily. It's left for Carry, Gerty and others to add to the portrait of this lady. Her minimalist allure is recognized by the arriviste Rosedale, who takes on a new dimension, expanding his own range, sometimes quite astutely, in the world that will not be able to withstand him for long. Able to read the signs of Lily's superior self-fashioning, he also sees in her the agency of his own revenge fantasy, to establish a woman, a consort who will grind his enemies underfoot. He knows she has enemies of her own. And for her part, Lily glimpses herself as a Pygmalion intrigued by the prospect of creating a Galatea. Nevertheless, she must abase herself to Bertha Dorset, because she can effect this transformation only within the closed world. Claustrophobia is revealed as well in Lily's lack of awareness, the need for other characters in the novel to describe her actions, however flippantly or contemptuously, and illuminate her motivations, whether actual or imagined, real or perceived.

What Lily does understand is that the distinction is moot. Blithely unconcerned about taking tea with Selden in his flat at the Benedick, she immediately regrets her act when accosted by Rosedale and, in her haste and anxiety, blurts out a careless and ill-conceived lie that compromises her future actions by clouding the innocence of the visit. At the end of Book I, Bertha Dorset's invitation to a Mediterranean cruise, ostensibly an escape, will actually narrow Lily's world and constrict her wing-span. Apparent salvation evolves into entrapment as Lily, brought along to distract George Dorset while his wife engages in an affair with Ned Silverton, stands accused by the adulteress of an indiscretion that compromises her standing in their set. Cast out of Eden, Lily understands the price of domicile among her enemies. Ecclesiastes might be a good text for Lily, given her fatalistic take on the world, but she is instead figured in the Book of Ruth. Reading Carry's role in their circle, she might be predicting her own future: 'It was, in fact, characteristic of Carry that, while she actively gleaned her own stores from the field of affluence, her real sympathies were on the other side – with the unlucky, the unpopular, the unsuccessful, with all her hungry fellow-toilers in the shorn stubble of success'. Lily is reduced to dependency on these fellow-exiles amid the alien corn, forced to seek comfort with the impoverished and the unlovely.

A friend reminded me of how small the Manhattan houses of even the very rich were at the beginning of the twentieth century, and he mentioned that Wharton lived on East Twenty-third Street, 'right where Madison Avenue empties out.' Wasn't that just above the horrible yuppie bar bought in the 1980s by a consortium of models and their managers, a true success story in the annals of New York real estate? Douglas thought not, so after a *prix-fixe* lunch at the Turkish Kitchen, we walked two blocks west and four blocks south. Sure enough, across the street from Madison Square Park, over Live Bait, with its windows filled with facetious and shabbified fishing props, he identified an unassuming flat yellow façade as that of Wharton's apartment. 'She'd write her pages in longhand and then pack them up and take them around the corner to her publisher on Broadway and East Nineteenth Street.' Down the block stands the Flatiron Building, New York's first skyscraper, which houses the offices of St. Martin's Press and Palgrave Macmillan, where I picked up and delivered freelance copy-editing work for years. Today it also contains MAC, Origins, and Jo Malone, a trio of upscale chain shops. The area has steadily polished its reputation over the last two decades and is probably already the next big destination neighborhood. I like to think that under Wharton's window there are young women with dreams and longings less resistant to realization than Lily Bart's, ambling, sauntering, and striding into their future.

Meet the Reading Group

The Monday Group
Ten heads are better than one

Marleen Hacquoil and Thelma Rondel

Our group – The Monday Group – started a little over 25 years ago after the original group completed an Adult Educational A-level English Literature course at Highlands College here in Jersey. Two of our original members are still active. The group consists of 10 members, all women, aged between 50 and 87 years. We meet every Monday afternoon and each choose our books for discussion over a period of one month (more or less, depending on the depth of and interest in the chosen book). In between, we have a collection of short stories, another of poetry and another of plays, to enjoy and discuss as interval reading. We started off this year with Caryl Churchill's *Top Girls*, before moving on to Rose Tremain's *Music and Silence*. We decided on E.M. Forster's *A Passage to India* over David Mitchell's *Cloud Atlas* as the next book for reading and discussion, favouring its straightforward style though no less enigmatic plot. It was a close decision, however, and *Cloud Atlas* will probably crop up again.

It was a rewarding surprise to find that *The Birds* by Aristophanes has as much contemporary relevance as it does. How many people who use the expression 'cloud cuckoo land' have the remotest idea that Aristophanes used it first 2400 years ago? There is so much humour, and far fewer puzzling references in *The Birds* than in his other comedies. One member of our group has acted in and produced plays and she was able to encourage us in the chorus and birdsong!

Regrettably, P.D. James, an intelligent writer who has given us much pleasure in the past, disappointed us with *The Murder Room*. It was not worthy of her reputation, to quote another of our group. We rarely read mysteries, and are unlikely to choose another by that author. In *Coriolanus* we found the roles of the women to be particularly compelling, especially the mother's relationship to her son. As we are all (with one exception) mothers, perhaps that was to be expected. The play also allowed us to vent our spleen over wars in general and Iraq in particular. Our sortie into the world of Les Murray's *Fredy Neptune* stretched our horizons, sending us scurrying to history books to learn more about the massacre of the Armenians during the First World War and about the personalities that dotted the Australian landscape throughout the century. Some of the Aussie expressions escaped us, and the work as a whole might have daunted us individually but with the support of the group we found it exhilarating.

The group doesn't always agree on everything; our discussions point up how wrong-headed some people can be in interpreting the author's intentions. But overall, ten heads are better than one.

The Monday Group's past reading includes:

Buddenbrooks – Thomas Mann
Middlesex – Jeffery Eugenides
The Summer Book – Tove Jansson
Coriolanus – William Shakespeare
The Sweetest Dream – Doris Lessing
The Idiot – Fyodor Dostoevsky
The Line of Beauty – Alan Hollinghurst
The Amateur Marriage – Anne Tyler
The Man Who Loved Children – Christina Stead
The Reader – Bernhard Schlink
The Merchant of Venice – William Shakespeare
Fredy Neptune – Les Murray
The Palace of Dreams – Ismail Kadare
The Curious Incident of the Dog in the Night Time – Mark Haddon

With selected 'interval reading' from:

The Art of the Story: An International Anthology of Contemporary Short Stories, ed. Daniel Halpern (Penguin, 2000)
Scanning the Century: The Penguin Book of the Twentieth Century in Poetry, ed. Peter Forbes (Penguin, 1999)
The Methuen Book of Modern Drama, Caryl Churchill, Sarah Kane, Mark Ravenhill (2003)

The Clutch of Earth

Seamus Heaney, *District and Circle*
Faber, 2006
ISBN 0-571-23096-2

Sarah Coley

Out walking, Heaney comes upon a nest at ground level:

On the Spot

A cold clutch, a whole nestful, all but hidden
In last year's autumn leaf-mould, and I knew
By the mattness and the stillness of them, rotten,
Making death sweat of a morning dew
That didn't so much shine the shells as damp them.
I was down on my hands and knees there in the wet
Grass under the hedge, adoring it,
Early riser busy reaching in
And used to finding warm eggs. But instead
This sudden polar stud
And stigma and dawn stone-circle chill
In my mortified right hand, proof positive
Of what conspired on the spot to addle
Matter in its planetary stand-off.

The eggs are dead, but his timing of the realisation is vague. 'A cold clutch,' he starts, then says 'and I knew…', so that as you read the poem that's what you know first of all too: the eggs are rotten, 'Making death sweat of a morning dew' (with that lovely cadence of the Metaphysical poets). But in fact, in real time, Heaney didn't know: 'I was down on my hands and knees there in the wet / Grass under the hedge, adoring it'. You can feel the eagerness in the line-ending, the inconvenience of wet grass that doesn't bother him at all, 'early riser busy reaching in…' The poem gathers force and changes tack entirely when the expected warm eggs are discovered cold, and 'on the spot' yields to the widest separation, 'Matter in its planetary stand-off'.

It's an emphatic and unearthly response to the cheat of life, and so here is the question: why does he say 'I knew' at the end of line two, as if there had been no shock and no reversal? Heaney has said that he wants 'to surprise himself with language' but here he seems – unlike himself – reluctant to be caught off guard, even though the surprise is let in so forcefully that it controls the poem at once. There is, in the best sense, a novel-like quality in Heaney's latest collection, a sense of necessary commitment to unclear positions. Why does he speak of 'stigma', a double blow, as if the removal of the hoped for new life were cause for shame? (For not holding on after the proof? For having hoped in the first place? For living beyond the loss?) At the centre of the poem there's the memory of himself *knowing*.

I keep thinking here of Wordsworth's sonnet, 'Surprised by joy', which opens with the paradoxical recovery of the poet being so moved by a sight or feeling that he forgets his three-year-old daughter is dead, and he turns to talk to her.

District and Circle is grounded by poems in memory of friends and family and poets, the recently dead and the long lost, his brother, his father, Czeslaw Milosz, Ted Hughes, George Seferis, Pablo Neruda, Edward Thomas, Dorothy and William Wordsworth. In 'Wordsworth's Skates', Heaney sees the actual skates on show behind glass, and they bring to his mind the lines from *The Prelude* where Wordsworth recalls his boyhood skating and the wheeling of the cliffs when he stopped short, 'even as if the earth had rolled / With visible motion her diurnal round'. The skates in Heaney's poem have two realities, both as a potential source of conjured life and as perished objects in the display case:

> Not the bootless runners lying toppled
> In dust in a display case,
> Their bindings perished,
>
> But the reel of them on frozen Windermere
> As he flashed from the clutch of earth along its curve
> And left it scored.

The 'bootless runners' (perfect ambiguity in the phrase) are inert and toppled items, undignified. You can go and look at them, and that might be all you get, a sign of moving no more, of being dead. But poetry does something more active than that. There's the flash and the escape from the 'clutch of earth': all that is a living exchange between writer and reader. The impermanent flash becomes a scored line. The presence of both the solid and the visionary is familiar throughout Heaney's work. What seems new here is the way they are placed by one another, lined up and separate. It's almost like a test. If the transformation of the ordinary is possible, as Wordsworth believed, as Heaney believes, *then go on, let's have the extraordinary.*

In 'To Mick Joyce in Heaven', Heaney offers a fantastic metaphor for the unrecoverable quality of an individual life:

> The weight of the trowel,
> That's what surprised me.
> You'd lift its lozenge-shaped
> Blade in the air
> To sever a brick
> In a flash, and then twirl it
> Fondly and lightly.
> But whenever you sent me
> To wash it and dry it
> And you had your smoke,
> Its iron was heavy,
> Its sloped-angle handle
> So thick-spanned and daunting
> I needed two hands.

The trowel that is bright and light in the air in Mick Joyce's hands,
is a dead weight when passed to the poet, 'So thick-spanned and
daunting / I needed two hands'. So much for elegy! A living figure
emerges that is yet as heroic and remote as the men in Heaney's
Beowulf. The life always was unrecoverable. But there's a direct
warmth when Heaney addresses the man outright: "'To Mick Joyce
in Heaven" – / The title just came to me, / Mick, and I started / If
not quite from nowhere, / Then somewhere far off'. This puts the
poem on track, and puts the poet right. The numinous is no longer
a gap in the poem but part of experience. 'I started… somewhere
far off'. What looks like a breach, *feels* like a journey. This is one of
the puzzles of particular movement. The more in place you are, the
more unsettled things are about to become.

I think this is what I've been skirting around saying. At a certain
age the deaths of friends must make you wonder about your own
death, almost as a temptation or as something that is growing familiar.
The three 'Found Prose' pieces are all like this. In the first, 'The Lagans
Road', Heaney remembers being a child going to school for the first
time, that absolute difference in experience, which in later years he
connects to a myth of the Pacific Northwest Indians about dying:

> coming along a forest path where other travellers' cast-
> offs lay scattered on the bushes, hearing voices laughing
> and calling, knowing there was a life in the clearing up
> ahead that would be familiar, but feeling at the same time
> lost and homesick – it struck me I had already experi-
> enced that kind of arrival.

In 'Tall Dames', the third of the prose pieces, he remembers the stir brought in by gypsy visitors, 'Every time they landed in the district, there was an extra-ness in the air, as if a gate had been left open in the usual life, as if something might get in or out.' I love that invisible line's end pause before 'or out' that makes the phrase lift. The gathering swallows in the third verse of 'Ode to Autumn' must have had such a feeling.

The best poems have got that 'extra-ness in the air':

Stern
in memory of Ted Hughes

'And what was it like,' I asked him,
'Meeting Eliot?'
　　　　　'When he looked at you,'
He said, 'It was like standing on a quay
Watching the prow of the *Queen Mary*
Come towards you, very slowly.'

　　　　　Now it seems
I'm standing on a pierhead watching him
All the while watching me as he rows out
And a wooden end-stopped stern
Labours and shimmers and dips,
Making no real headway.

The once-removed meeting with Eliot and the feeling that he is watching Hughes as he rows out, seem to converge in that dazzling sense of 'Making no real headway'.

There are magnificent poems in Heaney's twelfth collection; in particular, 'Tollund Man in Springtime' and 'The Lift', and the sequence 'Out of this World' written for Milosz. 'Saw Music' (from that sequence) is full of Milosz's dedication to this world. He 'lies this god-beamed day / Coffined in Krakow, as out of this world / Now as the untranscendent music of the saw / He might have heard in Vilnius and Warsaw // And would not have renounced, however paltry.' The ordinary cliché 'out of this world' unfurls with two-fold strength, and the bite in the last line is simply proud.

There are delicate moments of coincidence and missed meeting, as in the title poem, in which momentarily the poet thinks he sees his father's face in his own reflection on an underground train: 'My father's glazed face in my own waning / And craning'. The pull within the last three words is about as active a force as poetry can hold, the way the resemblance (or presence) rises more summoning as it retreats. Poems like this have, literally, a staying power.

Roadlessness

Peter Kocan, *Fresh Fields*
George MacDonald, *Phantastes*

Mary Weston

*F*resh Fields, the story of a young lad cast adrift in rural Australia in the early 1960s, is also a study of the imagination, one of the most interesting fictional portraits of the inner world I have read.

The main character is never named, referred to throughout the book as 'the youth'. This can be annoying stylistically, but it's worth putting up with for the constant sense of dissociation it imposes on the text. Even when we are privy to his most intimate thoughts, he is nameless. Is he nameless to himself? His mother and younger brother are also 'the woman' and 'the boy', though the abusive man they are escaping is called Vladimir. They are almost nobodies, and the perilous fragility of their existence is terrifying. 'What if he had seen them pull away in the taxi with the two suitcases? What if he was on the next train behind them? The youth had a continuous urge to look over his shoulder.' It's a relief for the reader when he is finally able to slip away from the bleakness of their temporary accommodation in the Shangri-La Private Hotel and enter his own mind:

> He couldn't think properly with other people near, couldn't lose himself in reflection the way he needed to. The youth liked to mutter his thoughts to himself to hear what they sounded like in words. Whenever he went too long without some private thinking-space he became off-balanced and anxious, as though all sorts of dangerous complications might be building up unnoticed. Only by continually thinking could he keep things under control.

The mainstay of his inner world is a character from a film, a Nazi fugitive through France in the last stages of the war. When life becomes too threatening, the youth can escape into 'the Diestl mood', actually pretending he is limping along with a Schmeisser submachine gun slung from his good shoulder, eyeing the inhabitants of these bush towns distrustfully, every one a potential enemy. Adopting this state of mind blocks any sense of the real terrors of his situation, the more effectively as the Diestl character

> has every feeling burnt out of him except for a sort of grim
> pride that will make him determined and dangerous until
> the moment he goes down. Maybe 'pride' was the wrong
> word. The youth didn't know what the right word was. All
> he knew was that the scenes of Diestl limping along like a
> wolf or an outlaw along the roads of a ruined and hostile
> world answered something deep in him.

This carefully balanced tone of objective sympathy allows us to experience the romance of this alienation without in any way seducing us to admire or fall into it (as for example Salinger and Camus do). We can see in fact that it's a bit cheesy. And yet the mechanism is more complex than James Bond wish-fulfilment fantasy. The imagination is speaking the truth even as it conceals it: there is a profound similarity in the two situations. Both are lonely, both are desperate. The Diestl fantasy demands a kind of aesthetic discipline, a truth to life, or it simply wouldn't be satisfying. And the imagination has its own laws of thermodynamics:

> The youth would have gone into the Diestl mood to make
> himself impervious to everything, but the Diestl mood
> was all used up for the moment. It was like an inner
> battery that needed time to recharge. He wished he could
> just go to sleep and not wake up until the battery was full
> again.

Diestl is not the only figure in his imagination. A picture of Grace Kelly catches his eye; 'Her poised self-containedness made him feel a bit more poised and self-contained himself. The youth had learnt that there were times when he needed 'a different kind of consolation from the sort Diestl gave.' Diestl's survival mechanism is absolute isolation and distrust of any other human being. But the youth also experiences an increasing need for connection, powered by sexuality. Diestl and Grace Kelly are antitheses: through his work with them both, and through the excruciatingly comical accidents and encounters and near misses of his real life, he arrives at a synthesis of genuine beauty and natural power, which he thinks of as 'The Great Reciprocation':

> It darted in as a thought about Romeo and Juliet. They had
> more passion and anguish than most people ever have.
> And therefore… they *provide* it for those people….
> Things like passion and skill and beauty and heroism

are granted to individual people, the youth reasoned, because the thing needs a person to embody it. In a much more important sense, through, those things belong to the entire human race. It was like someone being an excellent gardener and having gorgeous flowers in *their* yard. That the flowers are in their yard is just a kind of technicality, but that those flowers exist in the world is splendour of nature and a joy of the human spirit...

These concepts... armed him in a way he'd never known before. He began to see what a crude implement a Schmeisser was by comparison. He would have liked to confer with Diestl about it all, but he feared Diestl would be suspicious – especially of the bit about accepting joy as readily as disaster.

I happened to be reading George MacDonald's classic fairy tale *Phantastes* (first published in 1858), at about the same time as I was given *Fresh Fields* and found it illuminating to compare the two. The hero is another drifting young man – his name, Anodos, apparently means 'Roadless' in Greek. He is not homeless, however, but wandering through an alternative reality, Faerie. It is not only the character who wanders; unfortunately the plot has its false starts and pointless digressions, though the imagery these throw up is often so beautiful MacDonald can be forgiven for taking the scenic route. And of course the whole notion of fairies and Fairy Land is going to be difficult for us to accept. But it is worth wading through the treacle for what MacDonald has to say about nature and the imagination:

> Just as you could form some idea of the nature of a man from the kind of house he built, if he followed his own taste, so you could, without seeing the fairies, tell what any one of them is like, by looking at the flower till you feel that you understand it. For just what the flower says to you, would the face and form of the fairy say; only so much more plainly as a face and human figure can express more than a flower.

What are we doing when we personify plants or forces of nature? It's as if we need to portray reality to ourselves through a human or humanised image. Is it similar to the way the youth projects his situation onto Diestl? Are we falsifying reality, or somehow shaping it into a context that helps us to understand it?

> Why are all reflections lovelier than what we call the reality?...The commonest room is a room in a poem when I turn to the glass... In whatever way it may be

> accounted for, of one thing we may be sure, that this feeling is no cheat: for there is no cheating in nature and the simple unsought feelings of the soul. There must be a truth involved in it, though we may but in part lay hold of the meaning. Even the memories of past pain are delightful; and past delights, though beheld only through clefts in the grey clouds of sorrow, are lovely as Fairy Land... The moon, which is the lovelier memory or reflex of the down-gone sun, the joyous day seen in the faint mirror of the brooding night, had rapt me away.

The moon, glowing with borrowed light, is the prototypical symbol of Faerie Land. And Faerie itself is like the reflex image of the human imagination.

Peter Kocan's compassionate objectivity says 'here is a young person living in a fantasy world; here are his own lucid reflections on how imagination works in his life.' But MacDonald throws us directly into that world; we enter it sensuously, and the experience is rather like being cast into a Pre-Raphaelite painting.

But Anodos has his own moments of lucidity and his own psychological journey. It involves encountering his shadow, a literal shadow in the terms of the book, which perhaps shouldn't be equated too easily with Jungian ideas of the dark side of the self. Anodos' shadow has the effect of spoiling the beauty around him, disenchanting Fairy Land. He complains of being 'a man beside himself', a self-conscious spectator: the loss of the innocence that allows a child to enter wholeheartedly into the imaginative state. Perhaps this is meant to indicate a pseudo-sophisticated stage of life, in which Faerie is rejected as childish and unreal. Anodos has to suffer and achieve in order to expiate his pride and cynicism. For MacDonald, authenticity is directly linked to the imagination. This may seem counterintuitive, but isn't it true that the effect of reading fairy tales is to re-awaken a sense of wonder in the natural world, and to sensitise us to archetypal presences and processes in our inner lives?

"It was more bearable to do without tenderness for himself than to see that his own tenderness could make no amends for the lack of other things to her."

George Eliot, *Middlemarch*

More Than the Losses of My Life on Earth
The Poetry of James Wright

Ann Stapleton

> Yes, we need one another in deep, strange ways.
> James Wright

James Wright was born in 1927, in the industrial river town of Martins Ferry, Ohio, to a working-class family he described as 'very unpredictable, and rather wildly kind.' His father worked for fifty years at the Hazel-Atlas Glass Company, a fate that Wright, who loved and respected him, was nevertheless desperate to avoid. The poet Donald Hall, a longtime friend of Wright's, wrote that 'For no one more than James Wright was literature so much a choice of life over death: Thomas Hardy and Beethoven on the one hand; on the other hand Martins Ferry and Hazel-Atlas Glass [... Moreover, for Wright] poetry expressed and enacted compassion over the world's suffering.'

Wright was plagued by bipolar disorder, and at the age of sixteen lost a year of school to the first of many breakdowns he would endure throughout his life, involving electroshock treatments, extended hospitalizations, and at least one suicide attempt. In a letter to his ex-wife, he wrote, 'There's a place in E. A. Robinson that suggests how I felt for months: where he speaks of "some poor devil on a battlefield / Left undiscovered, and without the strength / To drag a maggot from his clotted mouth."' But if Wright's life was to a great degree shaped by his illness, even by the contours of its abeyance, he understood that, in order to survive, he would need to befriend it, that even though its repeated approaches would terrorize and deplete him, his madness would always come bearing powerful, strange gifts. If the chief work of Wright's poems is absolution, he extends it even to the impersonal energies of this world: a lightning storm in the sky (or a glitch in a poet's brain) does not intend the harm it can cause, and thereby is innocent, sometimes even exquisite, and so must be forgiven. He wrote to the poet Galway Kinnell

that 'the truth is there is something terrible, almost unspeakably terrible, in our lives, and it demands respect, and, for some reason that
seems to me quite insane, it doesn't hate us.' And he sent this hard-
won encouragement to a former student struggling with her own
illness: 'You'll have to find a way to be true to the depression, too,
because it has a place in our lives, somewhere.' A lesson not lost on
his son Franz, who has endured a similar struggle to survive mental
illness and the tendency toward self-medication that often comes
with it, while at the same time trying to keep the creative spirit alive.
Like his father, Franz received the Pulitzer Prize for poetry, making
the Wrights the only father and son winners in the award's history.

Though Wright was a distinctly American poet, some of his
most cherished 'imaginative resources' were products of the English
soil. He wrote his Ph.D. dissertation on Charles Dickens, whom
he especially loved for capturing 'better than anyone else [...] the
complete nuttiness of people,' both delightful and horrifying; para-
phrasing, he concurred with Santayana's thought that 'people who
think Dickens exaggerated are people who just don't know how to
pay attention.' Wright was particularly admiring of the novelist's
ability to convey a clear-eyed view of society's lunacy through the
innocence of a child's perception (Oliver Twist's perfectly natural
desire for more) or the psychosis of a madman (Wright considered
Barnaby Rudge 'a great and neglected novel'. For him, Barnaby's
madness – in much the same way a poet's does – actually reflects
the world's reality). 'Dickens has shaken me to the very bottom of
myself,' Wright confided to his doctoral advisor. 'I've had so many
poems begin after reading Dickens that I ought to send part of the
payment to his Estate.'

Wright also delighted in the works of Thomas Hardy, and prized
him for his tender awareness 'of the seriousness of life to those who
live it, and of the strangeness in which they have a share whether they
know it or not.' In a letter to the poet Richard Eberhart, Wright, for
the sheer joy of it, copied out a two-page description of *The Wood-
landers'* 'mysterious, green, unutterably beautiful character' Giles
Winterbourne, 'standing confused on a town street-corner with
his arm around an apple-tree that he's carrying along with him'. A
'miracle' Wright believed 'must have occurred to Hardy's imagination
as helplessly and overwhelmingly as a blossom occurs to a branch'.
He believed Hardy 'one of the most truly devout authors in English.'

And the loyal Wright's 'favorite poet in the world' was Edward
Thomas: 'A holy man, I believe, a saintly man' wrote Wright, calling
the Englishman 'one of the secret spirits who help keep us alive.' In
a letter to the American confessional poet Anne Sexton, he spoke of

a time of grief and self-hatred when he destroyed a very old, beloved copy of Whitman, tearing it to pieces and thrusting it

> down into the rankest mucky bottom sludge of an old garbage can near a dirty railroad track in Minneapolis; then I burned my manuscripts. Years of them. A symbolic suicide, if there ever was one.
>
> And yet – even when I planned, as often I did, to ignore 'symbols' and just get the job over and done with, I never even thought of destroying this book by Edward Thomas. It was always the book I loved best, and I read it only when I was true and real. And I guess that it has preserved my best self when nothing else was preserved by anyone, in any way, anywhere.

In a moving letter to the poet Robert Mezey, Wright, exhausted from another bruising round with his illness ('It was day and night of authentic nightmare'), describes his halting, openhearted attempt to make a poem out of his fear and sorrow (poetry was, at times, quite literally lifesaving):

> Well, here's my sonnet. It may not be much (I can't tell… I am in a hell of a shape, really); but it gave me another touch of secret joy which I needed very badly; because I love the art of the sonnet very much. It is about itself… i.e., the attempt to write a sonnet after long having lost touch with this noble form.

Midway through his career, Wright switched to free verse, but here, in his madness, he cleaves to his 'native rocks,' listening very hard for a song he has always known, one that is old and sacred, and might yet have the power to restore his life:

To Build a Sonnet

> I had not gone back there, because to go
> Meant pouring moonlight of a skinny kind
> On slag heap, that my mother used to know:
> Slow smoldering hell, shrunken, and hard to find.
> Now I have gone back there, it is no dream;
> It is broad waking; I have leave to go,
> But not of anybody's goodness now.
> It is my native rocks I go back to,
>
> And build a sonnet. Laboring as I hide
> Behind the shadow of this great hinge flung wide
> Where Clare, John Ransom, Robinson stepped forth,

> I lift my slight wall, yawing to one side,
> My spine a splinter between winds, yet worth
> More than the losses of my life on earth.

The following poem is among Wright's most famous, and perhaps infamous, as well, as so many English professors have debated the last line (some infuriated by it) and the nature of the moral Wright wished it to impart. But in fact, the poem is most remarkable for its ability to clear away the mind's usual apparatus of meaning (this stands for that, and that is really this) to make way for an interlude of pure being in that peaceful hour before the night returns, a little time in which to experience fully the serenity of needing nothing more than what you already have, and wanting to be no place on earth but where you are. The word 'wasted' in the last line refers to all the chances for such happiness the speaker, like each of us, has let go by.

Lying in a Hammock
at William Duffy's Farm
in Pine Island, Minnesota

Over my head, I see the bronze butterfly,
Asleep on the black trunk,
Blowing like a leaf in green shadow.
Down the ravine behind the empty house,
The cowbells follow one another
Into the distances of the afternoon.
To my right,
In a field of sunlight between two pines,
The droppings of last year's horses
Blaze up into golden stones.
I lean back, as the evening darkens and comes on.
A chicken hawk floats over, looking for home.
I have wasted my life.

Dylan Thomas wrote that 'The best craftsmanship always leaves holes and gaps [...] so that something that is not in the poem can creep, crawl, flash or thunder in,' and Wright's instinctive humility before the power of language, the magnanimity with which he accepts its continual refusal to yield up all of life's secrets to even the most ardent human study, is one of his great strengths as a poet. His stunning nature poems are really metaphysical pieces that make use of a very idiosyncratic animal imagery and sensory descriptions of life along the ground to access complicated, all but indescribable states of awareness. Consider 'Milkweed,' a poem that begins by

describing an intensely personal retrospection that is almost mystical, yet which somehow, as a direct result of the poem's quiet refusal
to explain itself, achieves a deep intimacy with the reader:

Milkweed

> While I stood here, in the open, lost in myself,
> I must have looked a long time
> Down the corn rows, beyond grass,
> The small house,
> White walls, animals lumbering toward the barn.
> I look down now. It is all changed.
> Whatever it was I lost, whatever I wept for
> Was a wild, gentle thing, the small dark eyes
> Loving me in secret.
> It is here. At a touch of my hand,
> The air fills with delicate creatures
> From the other world.

'Whatever it was' the speaker lost, the thing he 'wept for,' is a being
Wright is content to describe, but leave nameless. Our sense is of an
entity that somehow wished him well, that wanted him to live, but
his not being able to say for certain what it was is one of the bright
'holes' or 'gaps' to which Thomas refers, and what creeps shyly
through it into the poem is the reader's own sense of loss.

W.H. Auden, who in 1954 selected Wright's *The Green Wall* as
winner of the Yale Series of Younger Poets Award, wrote that 'Evil
is unspectacular and always human, and shares our bed and eats at
our own table,' and this recognition of kinship with the transgressor,
including the one that dwells within each of us, is a preoccupation of
Wright's. His poems speak for the wretched figure standing alone on
the gallows of his own mistakes, mourning his lost best self, already
dead and buried long ago. In 'At the Executed Murderer's Grave,'
if the tone is strident, it is meant to be. Wright does not offer us a
prayer for the killer George Doty, but 'a lament – a cursing lament,
the only real kind, the kind Heathcliff speaks to Cathy Linton on
her deathbed – for the real murderer, which is of course society and
– since I belong to society, since I didn't defend the human being in
the grave – a cursing lament for myself':

> I pity myself because a man is dead.
> If Belmont County killed him, what of me?
> His victims never loved him. Why should we?
> And yet, nobody had to kill him either.
> It does no good to woo the grass, to veil
> The quicklime hole of man's defeat and shame.

Nature-lovers are gone. To hell with them.
I kick the clods away, and speak my name.

The last line emphasizes that it is Wright's, the speaker's, everyone's
grave we look down on, and that the poor, deluded face peering out
of it is our own.

The poem includes this epigraph from Sigmund Freud: 'Why
should we do this? What good is it to us? Above all, how can we do
such a thing? How can it possibly be done?' But rather than being
the commentary on capital punishment most readers assume this
to be, the questions are, in fact, Freud's attempt to puzzle out the
(to him, 'staggering' and incomprehensible) idea of The Golden
Rule: knowing what he knew of human psychology, the idea that we
would attempt to do unto others as we would have them do unto us
was astonishing to him.

In 'Saint Judas,' Wright combines these two ideas – sympathy
for the one cast out of all human fellowship, and wonder at the true
miracle of any man's pity for another. Judas, he writes:

> placed himself beyond the moral pale, and he realized
> this. I've always been strongly moved by his hanging
> himself. Why did he do it? You would think he'd be a
> completely cold person. And yet, he couldn't have been
> to experience such complete despair. I tried to imagine
> what Judas was like.

Saint Judas

When I went out to kill myself, I caught
A pack of hoodlums beating up a man.
Running to spare his suffering, I forgot
My name, my number, how my day began,
How soldiers milled around the garden stone
And sang amusing songs; how all that day
Their javelins measured crowds; how I alone
Bargained the proper coins, and slipped away.

Banished from heaven, I found this victim beaten,
Stripped, kneed, and left to cry. Dropping my rope
Aside, I ran, ignored the uniforms:
Then I remembered bread my flesh had eaten,
The kiss that ate my flesh. Flayed without hope,
I held the man for nothing in my arms.

The 'for nothing' in the last line is ambiguous, meaning for no payment,
and also for no reason, as mercy cannot be bought or explained; it

simply is or is not, and it is always in our (damaged) hands.

In the poem 'Hook,' the dejected speaker, standing on a windy winter street corner in St. Paul, Minnesota, no bus expected for hours, is approached by a stranger:

> Then the young Sioux
> Loomed beside me, his scars
> Were just my age.
>
> Ain't got no bus here
> A long time, he said.
> You got enough money
> To get home on?

The rescuer, his hand revealed in 'the terrible starlight' to be only a silver hook, offers the speaker all he can spare:

> Did you ever feel a man hold
> Sixty-five cents
> In a hook,
> And place it
> Gently
> In your freezing hand?
>
> I took it. It wasn't the money I needed.
> But I took it.

And this is the blood money of Wright's Judas, those wages of a betrayal that always necessarily includes the self, returning now to the sinner's hand, but this time, they are transformed by human love in one of its many odd disguises. They bring with them the power to cleanse and to redeem, another kind of Judas kiss altogether, with the meaning of the word 'conviction' altered from 'a finding of guilt' to its other incarnation: 'a belief held firmly.'

Brush Fire

> In this field,
> Where the small animals ran from a brush fire,
> It is a voice
> In the burned weeds, saying
> I love you.
> Still, when I go there,
> I find only two gray stones,
> And, lying between them,
> A dead bird the color of slate.
> It lies askew in its wings,

Its throat bent back as if at the height of some joy too great
To bear to give.
And the lights are going out
In a farmhouse, evening
Stands, in a gray frock, silent, at the far side
Of a raccoon's grave.

The 'small animals' running from death, the voice 'saying I love you'
'in the burned weeds,' the 'dead bird the color of slate' are all images of
a human grief that has come true in the animal world. It is the killed
creature, the lost flight, of a deep love; the 'slate' of its body and the
'gray' of the evening's frock are the colors of a long day, a lost time,
that is ended. These are the realities of ash, of a deeply, irrevocably
altered (emotional) landscape, so changed that it is hardly recogniz-
able. Still, 'to bear' and 'to give' stand bravely, next to each other, as the
equals they always mean to be: we must somehow manage to do both,
and we must try to live. 'The lights' of something rare and beautiful
and never to come again 'are going out' (one of Wright's gaps – you
say what the something is; the farmhouse is only a stand-in for what
you loved that is going dark now as you watch). So much is happening
here, away from the light, where the pity of the houses cannot reach.
The evening's frock (daring throwback word to an olden time before
this ruined now) is gray and all is silent – not at all the perfect peace of
Duffy's farm in its radiant hour of gold, but the quiet of no words at all,
ending distantly 'at the far side of a raccoon's grave.' Of course, there's
no such thing as that, and yet, in those last four words, so impractical
that you can receive them in nothing but utter seriousness, you look
around you at all the strange burials in life that go unseen and unre-
marked, and unmemorialized by anything but night falling, and you
are made to mourn, for its brightness, the whole burned world.

In 'The Lambs on the Boulder,' a luminous short prose piece,
Wright takes as his starting point an exhibition of masterpieces
– from Giotto, 'the master of angels,' to Mantegna, whose dead
Christ 'looks exactly like a skidroad bum fished by the cops out of
the Mississippi in autumn just before daylight and hurried off in a
tarpaulin-shrouded garbage truck and deposited in another tangle
of suicides and befuddled drunkards at the rear entrance to the
University of Minnesota medical school.' This is the true Christ of
the Ohio River, the failed saviour whose loneliness draws Wright
to him. But of even greater interest to Wright than the exhibition is
what Wright calls 'a littler glory that I love best. It is a story, which
so intensely ought to be real that it is real,' the tale of the medieval
master painter Cimabue who, while walking in the country, pauses

to observe the young shepherd boy Giotto using a pebble 'to scratch sketches of his lambs on a boulder at the edge of the field.' Wright reveals that one of his 'idle wishes [as ever, he is modest; the wish is a devout one] is to find that field where Cimabue stood in the shade and watched the boy Giotto scratching his stone with his pebble':

> I would not be so foolish as to prefer the faces of the boy's lambs to the faces of his angels. One has to act his age sooner or later.
> Still, this little planet of rocks and grass is all we have to start with. How pretty it would be, the sweet faces of the boy Giotto's lambs gouged, with infinite and still uncertain and painful care, on the side of a boulder at the edge of a country field. [...]
> I wonder where that boulder is. I wonder if the sweet faces of the lambs are still scratched on its sunlit side. [...]
> In one of the mature Giotto's greatest glories, a huge choir of his unutterably beautiful angels are lifting their faces and are becoming the sons of the morning, singing out of pure happiness the praises of God.
> Far back in the angelic choir, a slightly smaller angel has folded his wings. He has turned slightly away from the light and lifted his hands. You cannot even see his face. I don't know why he is weeping. But I love him best.
> I think he must be wondering how long it will take Giotto to remember him, give him a drink of water, and take him back home to the fold before it gets dark and shepherd and sheep alike lose their way in the darkness of the countryside.

In the Wright cosmology, with belief turned upside down, with the dead skidroad Christ so badly in need of our forgiveness, and the task of love placed squarely on the shoulders of the human beasts, it is the boy Giotto who bears responsibility for the angel arisen from his need; it is the grieving angel who must wait forever for a mortal's slow return. And it is because of the terrible darkness propping up that sunward boulder wherever we left it so long ago ('I wonder where the stone is. I will never live to see it'), the lambs' faces still looking after us with such love in their eyes, that we seem sometimes, in all our tarnish, halfway golden, and love limps homeward, in all its lostness, to be found.

All Things That Live
Phoebe Hesketh (1909–2005)

Neil Curry

Reading Phoebe Hesketh's early poems – her first collection, *Lean Forward, Spring!* was published in 1948 – the term 'nature poet' inevitably comes to mind. At the same time, however, there is a *but* constantly hovering over it, which sometimes reminds us of the darker side there is to the poems of Robert Frost. This darkness is there even when her observation is at its most descriptive and precise, as, for example, when she writes:

> A ladybird
> Slides like a blood-drop down a spear of grass.

I have no doubt that blades of grass (consider the primary meaning of *blade*) have been compared to spears before, but never quite like this.

I suppose one of the reasons for this darker tone is that it is her own rather dour and sometimes foreboding northern landscape which she not only shows us, but which she uses, as in a particularly fine poem, 'Wordsworth's Old Age', where the landscape and the man become one:

> Cold is the rock face, moss and lichen banished
> To green forgotten springs locked deep below
> A frozen crust; the celandine has vanished.
> Where star and violet shone now falls the snow.

And of course it is not only the celandine here which skilfully reminds us of one of Wordsworth's early poems; the star and the violet had once been at the centre of that most lyrical and impassioned of the Lucy poems.

Throughout her 60-year career Phoebe Hesketh was always able to light up a poem with images which were strikingly apt and new, but never contrived, as in 'Cats':

> A fist of pins;
> Kettles on the purr
> Ready to spit.

And, because the combination is so unlikely yet so right, one of my favourites is simply 'prawn-whiskered barley'.

And her images were by no means all visual. She employed each of her senses and the result was not always pretty; she was sometimes capable of a physicality which makes you gag:

> I swallowed resentment
> Like hairs.

Her poetry was, in another sense, becoming increasingly *sensuous*, but in the 1970s, what had appeared to be foreboding in her outer landscape began to come threateningly closer. In 'He Saved Others...' she had written a moving elegy for her father, A. E. Rayner, the pioneering radiologist, and again it is her use of imagery which is so impressive. It was through his life – his lifelong love of mountaineering – that she makes us experience the suffering he went through at his death:

> From his hot white tent
> he peers at us faraway children, struggles to reach
> out and save, but the rope of speech
> frays in twitching fingers.
> He slips back into a whispering valley,
> groping for a ledge of comfort.

We must all at some time expect the death of our parents, but nothing can ever prepare us for the sudden death of a child and when her young son, Richard, was tragically drowned she was perhaps quite unable to tell us how she felt. Instead, in a poem of moving reticence and economy and with a logic which shocks, she has the boy himself tell us what it was like to die.

Boy Drowning

> Drowning is pushing through
> a barrier like birth
> only the elements are exchanged:
> air for water.
> Then water for air,
> my lungs
> folded flat as butterflies' wings
> struggled to expand
> in a round scream.
>
> Now I make no sound –
> or they don't hear

water drumming my ear-
drums, nostrils, eyes –
I fight like a salmon on grass
choked with a bubble.
I cannot rise
a third time.

That is one of the most courageous pieces of writing I know.

The religious implications of those closing lines were a pointer towards the direction she was about to take. 'Awareness sharpens with the shortening days' she wrote in 'Comparison with a Sunflower', and again 'All things that live are preparing to leave'. She considers the prospect of her own leaving with honest uncertainty and, as one would expect, not a glimmer of sentimentality. 'Survival' concludes with the lines:

Thus, united hand-in-hand
With death, life munches on.

Reviewing her 1977 collection *Preparing to Leave*, A. Alvarez wrote in *The Observer* that 'she has been absurdly underrated'. It may well be that she has been underrated by people who study poetry, but I doubt if she will ever be underrated by those who read it.

> yes, in spite of all,
> Some shape of beauty moves away the pall
> From our dark spirits. Such is the sun, the moon,
> Trees old and young, sprouting a shady boon
> For simple sheep; and such are daffodils
> With the green world they live in.

John Keats, *Endymion*

Journey of a Soul

Mrs Gaskell, *Ruth*

Denise Cottrell-Boyce

I loved reading *Ruth*. I started it when my baby was five months old and I planned to meander gently through the book in odd interludes and the ten minutes' quiet before bed. But before long I was letting him stay for hours on the breast, so that I could read just one more page, just one more page. When I should have been banking sleep against the interrupted nights ahead, I would just finish the chapter and then somehow find I had slipped into the next one. I dispensed with all non-functional conversation with my husband and ever so slightly resented the time I spent reading *The Wolves of Willoughby Chase* to my older children.

I was ensnared by a plot which is as simple as a Country and Western ballad – a friendless young girl is made pregnant by a heartless seducer. The story is told in a prose style of such beauty and clarity that I (who am inclined to race full pelt to completion) repeatedly stopped to re-read. Look at this description of a bedroom:

> After tea, Miss Benson took her upstairs to her room. The white dimity bed and the walls, stained green, had something of the colouring and purity of effect of a snowdrop; while the floor, rubbed with a mixture that turned it a rich dark brown, suggested the idea of the garden-mould out of which the snowdrop grows.

Above all, the psychological and spiritual illumination of the heroine's character make *Ruth* not merely the story of a life, but the journey of a soul. Apart from being pretty, Ruth is not a particularly charismatic figure in the early chapters. She has captured neither the interest of her guardian nor the affection of her peers, nor the devotion of her lovers. But by the end of the book her name is spoken with reverence by all who know her:

> Immediately there arose a clamour of tongues, each with some tale of his mother's gentle doings, till Leonard grew dizzy with the beatings of his glad, proud heart...[he]

> tried to speak, but for an instant he could not, his heart
> was too full: tears came before words, but at length he
> managed to say:
>> 'Sir, I am her son!'
>> 'Thou! Thou her bairn! God bless you, lad,' said an old
> woman, pushing her way through the crowd...
>> Many other wild and woebegone creatures pressed
> forward with blessings on Ruth's son, while he could only
> repeat:
>> 'She is my mother.'

From her own experience of working with 'fallen women', Mrs Gaskell would have been very aware that most of them were actually more like 'stumbling girls'. The uncomplicated story of Ruth's downfall employs many clichés – the orphaned girl, the heartless guardian, the rapacious employer and the faithless, rich seducer. In championing such a heroine one almost feels that Mrs Gaskell is abandoning her usual moral rigour: every one is to blame for Ruth's condition but Ruth herself. In a penny dreadful, Ruth would have finished herself off in the Welsh brook and much remorse would be felt by all. But here we are in reality and Ruth is not allowed such a swift exit. She must live on and earn her own salvation, step by plodding step. Nor is she to be one of Hardy's 'Ruined Maids' ('We never do work when we're ruined, said she'). In the symbolism of Christian baptism, immersion in water represents a drowning death from which the candidate emerges to new life in Christ. Ruth is drawn back from drowning herself by Thurston Benson and her new life begins.

> He thought of every softening influence of religion
> which over his own disciplined heart had power, but put
> them aside as useless. Then the still small voice whis-
> pered, and he spake:
>> 'In your mother's name, whether she be dead or alive,
> I command you to stay here until I am able to speak to
> you.'
>> She knelt down at the foot of the sofa, and shook it
> with her sobs.

Mrs Gaskell makes it abundantly clear that it is not rebuke and condemnation that brings about this reorientation in Ruth's life but acceptance, succour and, above all, affection. In the moral stance of Mr Benson and his sister, we find the voice of Christ – uncompromising to both condemner and condemned. Those who would judge are told, 'let he who is without sin cast the first stone' (John 8:7). But with equal rigor, the sinner is told, 'go and sin no more'. (John 8:11). In the unfolding story of *Ruth*, sin, ignorance and poverty of spirit are not swept away but systematically defeated by study, industry and above all, love. Love in all its manifestations is the virtue which illuminates this novel – maternal, fraternal, philanthropic but, above all, divine love. This is the wellspring of Ruth's regeneration, an inspiration to her benefactors, and the power from which all her strength is drawn. It is most manifest at the climax of the book when Ruth – her status enhanced by learning, grace and beauty – is offered that prize which to Victorian sensibility is a perfect solution to her social predicament: the heartless seducer proposes marriage. Ruth's tempestuous struggle with her soul is followed by an outpouring of grace and a surge of spiritual strength which elevate her beyond the reach of her worthless lover:

> She shut her eyes, until through the closed lids came a ruddy blaze of light. The clouds had parted away, and the sun was going down in the crimson glory behind the distant purple hills… Ruth forgot herself in looking at the gorgeous sight. She sat up gazing, and, as she gazed, the tears dried on her cheeks; and, somehow, all human care and sorrow were swallowed up in the unconscious sense of God's infinity. The sunset calmed her more than words, however wise and tender, could have done. It even seemed to give her strength and courage; she did not know how or why, but so it was.

In writing the story of Ruth's moral regeneration, Mrs Gaskell challenges contemporary nineteenth-century values with the values of the Gospel. A fitting epitaph for Ruth would be the prayer of exultation proclaimed by Mary (Luke 1:46-53): 'My soul magnifies the Lord and my spirit rejoices in God my saviour. For He who is mighty has done great things for me and holy is his name. He has scattered the proud in the imagination of their hearts and exalted the lowly. He has filled the hungry with good things. The Rich he has sent away empty.'

Reader, I started *Ruth* expecting a long read interrupted by the distractions of exhaustion, new babyhood, family, but in the great tradition of perfect reads I couldn't put it down. My baby was five months old when I started the book, and five-and-a-half months old when I finished it.

Good Books

Have you read any good books recently? Tell us – answers on a postcard – about your all-time favourite book, a great book you've read recently, or simply the book you're reading at the moment. Many thanks to Lesley Johnson and Helen Robey for this issue's contributions.

J. L. Carr, A Month in the Country
Lesley Johnson

As a novel, A Month in the Country (1980) is faultless, beautifully written and atmospheric (set in North Yorkshire of the 1920s). It is *just* the right length – not overblown as so many of today's stories tend to be.

Good Books,
The Reader,
19 Abercromby Square,
Liverpool,
L69 7ZG

Vikram Seth, *An Equal Music*
Helen Robey

Seth takes us into the world of classical music, through the story of Michael, a violinist in a quartet, and his reunion with his lost love, Julia, a concert pianist confronting deafness. I love the way the author conveys the almost mystical absorption of the musicians' minds in the music itself; and I shall always remember the lone violinist playing *The Lark Ascending* on Blackstone Edge.

Good Books,
The Reader,
19 Abercromby Square,
Liverpool,
L69 7ZG

The Best Physick

Daniel Defoe, *A Journal of the Plague Year*

Jean Edmunds

A little girl is being passed down from an upper window to a group of people standing in the street. Grass grows between the paving stones. Everyone looks hurried and anxious. As a child, I was fascinated by this scene depicted in a bound volume of the weekly *Chatterbox*, a relic of my father's Edwardian boyhood. During the Great Plague of 1665, children in particular would be sneaked out of sealed, plague-ridden houses and taken to the relative safety of the country. So many people left the city or died that parts of London appeared empty.

As England's first real novelist, Daniel Defoe is best known for his island survival story, *Robinson Crusoe*. The fictional *A Journal of the Plague Year* reads like an on-the-spot account but was published in 1772, some sixty years after the events narrated. It influenced H. G. Wells' *War of the Worlds*, where the narrator journeys through an almost empty Martian-invaded London:

> As the Desolation was greater, during those terrible Times, so the Amazement of the People encreas'd: and a thousand unaccountable Things they would do in the violence of their Fright…

Defoe recounts stories of horror, religious faith and lack of it, courage and endurance, villainy and betrayal, and of loyalty. The numbers of deaths recorded in each London parish (many went unrecorded) appear throughout the book like the marks of a tide rising slowly to flood proportions before finally receding.

His narrator is simply given as 'H.F.', initials thought to be borrowed from a Defoe uncle. (The family name was Foe but Daniel added the 'De' in an attempt to improve his social status.) H. F. stays in the city to protect his livelihood and the members of his household, and he does survive while pointing out that 'the best Physick against the Plague is to run away from it'. King Charles II and his court prudently decamped to Oxford. As with New Orleans in 2005, the better-off inhabitants had the means to depart.

H. F. lived 'without Aldgate about mid-way between Aldgate Church and White-Chappel-Bars'. Early in the outbreak the disease had not reached this side of the city, but

> at the other End of the Town, their Consternation was very great; and the richer sort of People, especially the Nobility and Gentry from the West-part of the City throng'd out of Town with their Families and Servants in an unusual Manner... Indeed nothing was to be seen but Waggons and Carts, with Goods, Women, Servants, Children, etc. Coaches fill'd with People of the Better Sort, and Horsemen attending them.

Not all were wealthy. One story concerns a group of three men, a former sailor, an ex-soldier and a carpenter, who ventured into the countryside. Though finding themselves shunned by most villagers and small-town folk, these practical fellows coped well, befriending other refugees along the way and returning at last to the chastened city. Many other citizens took to the river, and sat out the crisis aboard ship, letting down baskets to collect provisions brought by relatives and friends in small boats.

No one in the seventeenth century knew what caused the illness or how it was transmitted. It wasn't known until the plague bacillus *Yersina pestis* was discovered at the time of the 1844 Hong Kong epidemic. We know now, of course, that bubonic plague is carried by fleas on brown rats (though the bacillus itself can survive in faeces or bedding and clothing for up to a year if conditions are warm and damp).

Nobody *then* had a clue how to prevent the plague, protect themselves against it, or treat it. Wild theories abounded. Quacks and charlatans made fortunes deceiving people into 'wearing Charms, Philters, Exorcisms, Amulets, and I know not what Preparations, to fortify the Body with them against the Plague; as if the Plague was not the Hand of God, but a kind of a Possession of an evil Spirit'.

The word *Abracadabra*, today just an amateur magician's cliché, was taken very seriously. Written out in inverted pyramid form, from the full word to a lone A, it was regarded as an important charm.

The image most associated with the plague is of crosses marked on doors where the illness had struck, and carts trundling about to cries of 'Bring out your dead!', but the feeling of documentary realism is underscored as Defoe emphasises that 'Provisions were always to be had in full Plenty, and the Price not much rais'd neither' and 'No dead bodies lay unburied or uncovered, no Funeral or sign of it was to be seen in the Daytime'.

Journal of a Plague Year in one sense feels a modern book in that it relates closely to natural disasters such as the 1918 Spanish flu pandemic and, more recently, the Boxing Day tsunami of 2004, or the New Orleans flood and the Pakistani earthquakes of 2005. Above all it is a fascinating account of human behaviour in a time of stress.

A Timeless Heroine

Michele A. Sweeten

Sometimes I come across a heroine who resonates to my core, whose relationship with me through the page can shore up my flagging resolve, who reaches across the traffic, television, and travesty of my daily life and really... connects. She is one who, sinking into her own poor choices, meets the rising tide of consequences with a failing sense of strength and a small reserve of stubbornness that somehow carries her through. Though it feels like a victory, its source is mysterious enough to promote wonderment rather than pride.

Helen Huntingdon of Anne Brontë's *The Tenant of Wildfell Hall* is a heroine whose naïvety and idealism of youth meet with the smooth-talking charisma of a young man exactly the opposite of the 'really good man' that her guardians desire her to marry:

> 'Well, my dear, ask your uncle what sort of company he keeps, and if he is not banded with a set of loose, profligate young men, whom he calls his friends – his jolly companions, and whose chief delight is to wallow in vice, and vie with each other who can run fastest and farthest down the headlong road to the place prepared for the devil and his angels...
>
> Oh, Helen, Helen! You little know the misery of uniting your fortunes to such a man!'

How many of us have not heard some sage prophecy from a relative or friend, whose vision of the forest fell on deaf ears as we joyously examined the bark kissing the end of our noses? Helen is convinced that her fervent faith and righteous upbringing will mend any small fissures in the lover's character. She even arms herself with the popular psychology of our own day, that if a person's upbring-

ing has been harsh or abusive, at no point does their bad behaviour
become their own fault:

> I long to deliver him from his faults – to give him an
> opportunity of shaking off the adventitious evil got from
> contact with others worse than himself, and shining out
> in the unclouded light of his own genuine goodness – to
> do my utmost to help his better self against his worse, and
> make him what he would have been if he had not, from the
> beginning, had a bad, selfish, miserly father, who, to gratify
> his own sordid passions, restricted him in the most inno-
> cent enjoyments of childhood and youth, and so disgusted
> him with every kind of restraint; – and a foolish mother
> who indulged him to the top of his bent, deceiving her
> husband for him, and doing her utmost to encourage those
> germs of folly and vice it was her duty to suppress…

What a rude awakening she receives! Even before the wedding
date, she confesses to her diary:

> My cup of sweets is not unmingled: it is dashed with a
> bitterness that I cannot hide from myself, disguise it as
> I will… I cannot shut my eyes to Arthur's faults; and the
> more I love him the more they trouble me.

After one year, she admits that her 'bliss is sobered… hopes diminished and fears increased, but not yet thoroughly confirmed'. After
another year, 'I spared him my exhortations and fruitless efforts at
conversion too, for I saw it was all in vain'. Eventually, her passion
for him is stabbed to death when, in the garden, she unwittingly
comes upon Arthur with another woman, proclaiming his undying
love for the supplanter, and his utter lack of love for his own wife.

That Helen finds her strength gone in this moment is expected,
that she discovers her faith (flamed consistently by the daily application of its tenets to her struggling heart) available is redemption
even for us. It bolsters the hope that we too can daily think and act
in such a way as to build an unseen force ready to meet fear itself.

Helen's greatest victory over the consequences of her own
actions is yet to come: after escaping from her unfaithful husband,
the father of her young son, Helen chooses to go back to nurse the
ungrateful beast back to health after a terrible illness. Her concerned
friends can only wonder at her calling:

> 'Why did she take this infatuated step? What fiend
> persuaded her to it?'
> 'Nothing persuaded her but her own sense of duty.'

It is certain that Arthur himself does not see her actions as pure:

> 'Oh! I see,' said he, with a bitter smile, 'it's an act of Christian charity, whereby you hope to gain a higher seat in heaven for yourself, and scoop a deeper pit in hell for me.'

Does Helen act from selfishness? She is certainly conflicted. The torrent of opposing needs – of her impressionable young son, of her ailing and needy husband, of her own suffering heart – leads her down one path – escape – and then back again. This is a seldom vaunted brand of courage: the courage to change your mind. Everyone can question our motives, as Arthur does Helen's, but in the end our purposes are revealed by the fire of trial. If Helen believes that 'the fire will test each one's work, of what sort it is' (I Corinthians 3:13), and that 'the genuineness of your faith is tested by fire' (I Peter 1:7), then her choice to return to her abusive husband is an effort to put her own faith to the test.

Her test is our gain:

> I myself have had, indeed, but few incentives to what the world calls vice, but yet, I have experienced temptations and trials of another kind, that have required, on many occasions, more watchfulness and firmness to resist, than I have hitherto been able to muster against them. And this, I believe, is what most others would acknowledge, who are accustomed to reflection, and wishful to strive against their natural corruptions.

Helen does not see the precious metal of her soul as a finished work. She views herself as always digging in the pocket to balance the account, and coming up short. But she keeps digging, as we must.

> "Lydgate's discontent was much harder to bear; it was the sense that there was a grand existence in thought and effective action lying about him, while his self was being narrowed into the miserable isolation of egoistic fears and vulgar anxieties for events that might allay such fears."

George Eliot, *Middlemarch*

Ask the Reader

Q In this week's Sunday newspaper I read a review of a new biography of Flaubert which pointed out that he was epileptic. Well, nothing but sympathy, but it crossed my mind to wonder why so many great writers were physically or, more often, mentally afflicted. Doesn't that cut them off from the normal, sports-mad, fun-loving, healthy individual?

A Well now, 'sports-mad' is fine and 'fun-loving' understandable, but 'normal' I simply can't swallow. It implies a judgement derived from statistics which enforces a simple ghostly model upon that final word in your question, the individual who is precious precisely because unique. Let's admit instead that there is for all of us, even the afflicted, something you could call normal time, the routines of life. These would of course include playing, whether it's croquet or the cello, and fun, found in clubbing or reading the odes of Horace. Normalities vary with the individual but they are repeatable experiences, as are the emotions that attend them, the expected varieties of pleasure and disappointment. But they belong to an order of existence which long-term memory does not bother to record for that very reason and on which stories cannot be built. What our memories seize upon are more critical moments of intenser delight or more daunting sorrow, especially actually the latter in so far as, regrettably, fear is a stronger impulse than hope. Often we are not even conscious of the passage of normal time but special time takes us by surprise, though it lurks somewhere in our minds because when we enter it we often recognise that we have been there before. It's special time we need to keep in touch with and literature has always been the means to do so. A writer's vulnerabilities, physical or mental, may keep him or her in touch with such occasions, better able to comprehend them than we healthy folk and so ready to assist us whenever normal time deserts us, but more especially as a reminder while it's soothingly present.

Let me offer an example. When Tennyson's friend and intended brother-in-law Arthur Henry Hallam was suddenly killed by a stroke at the age of twenty-two, the effect was to prostrate the poet with grief, the more intense because morbid depression was a family inheritance. The result, of course, was his series of elegies later published as *In Memoriam*. Even when he apparently recovered from the paroxysms of grief he went on writing as though he were still feeling it. It's not just that in bereavement it's 'normal' to feel guilt over our powers of recuperation nor even that sudden bursts of sorrow overtake us amid an otherwise contented existence; it's that actually we don't want to lose our grief because in doing so we lose the lost person all over again. All that is the experience of 'normal' people, though we forget it often. Tennyson's friend, Edward Fitzgerald, he of the *Rubaiyat*, thought the whole business unhealthy ('I felt that if Tennyson had got on his horse and ridden twenty miles…he would have been cured of his sorrows in half the time'), and he argued against publication. What ensured the popularity of the poem was not only its struggle to believe that the value of the individual life was guaranteed by its immortality but also must have included what you would think was discomfiting to the 'normal healthy' reader; such as the constant talking to oneself, the discovery of multiple identities, even such fantasies as expecting the dead man not to realise he is dead and offer consolation to his grieving friend. In special time we are all a little mad; excess overtakes even the most reasonable person. So, to take at least one of your 'afflictions', there is no precise and constant division between mental health and its opposite. Indeed the willingness to admit to consciousness the chattering of the goblins that occurs at moments of crisis may deprive them of much of their malignity:

> I sometimes hold it half a sin
>   To put in words the grief I feel;
>   For words, like Nature, half reveal
> And half conceal the Soul within.
>
> But, for the unquiet heart and brain,
>   A use in measured language lies;
>   The sad mechanic exercise,
> Like dull narcotics, numbing pain.
>
> In words, like weeds, I'll wrap me o'er,
>   Like coarsest clothes against the cold:
>   But that large grief which these enfold
> Is given in outline and no more.
>   (*In Memoriam* V)

We need more Shakespeare and Tennyson and less Valium, and I look forward to the day when the GP will prescribe *King Lear* or bits of *Don Juan* or *The Waste Land* as sovereign remedies for our ills.

Newman's Notes

In the Grip of Light
Philip Larkin (I)

Stephen Newman

L arkin's most celebrated pronouncement on his poetry is probably: 'Deprivation is for me what daffodils were to Wordsworth'.
It's so witty you don't take it seriously. But it encapsulates the paradox
of Larkin's achievement. The beauty of his poetry is necessarily and
inextricably linked to the 'negativity' – the self-abnegation – of his
statements. Without the austerity of the life the poetry would not
exist. The transcendent light that irradiates and expunges the gloom
of the statements is directly consequent on the terrifying act of
letting go of the self. The fertility depends absolutely on the futility.

Fertility is not a word often associated with Larkin, but its
implications are everywhere. He is the poet of light, landscape,
heavy harvests and laughing Ceres. Wheat, the symbol of plenty,
crops up again and again: 'Its postal districts packed like squares of
wheat', 'Shadowing Domesday lines / Under wheat's restless silence',
'fast-shadowed wheat fields running high as hedges', 'Wind-muscled
wheatfields wash round villages'. This is not the Britain of the Welfare
State. It is as though an immensely more fastidious Walt Whitman
had found himself hurrahing in harvest.

As well as harvests there are the greatest landscapes in art since
Constable and Turner. The 'lit-up galleries' of 'Absences'; 'The piled
gold clouds' and 'Luminously-peopled air' of 'Here'; the cavernous,
wind-picked sky of 'Sad Steps'; 'that high-builded cloud' in 'Cut
Grass'; the 'big sky' that 'Drains down the estuary like the bed / Of a
gold river' in 'Livings'; even 'The sky is white as clay' in 'Aubade'.

Above all he is the poet of Time – not so much the destroyer as
in Hardy but the preserver. This is most apparent in 'The Whitsun
Weddings', a poem in which time has a sensuous palpable presence:
'All windows down, all cushions hot, all sense / Of being in a hurry
gone'. The summer day drowses in stupefying sunlight, recorded in

the blinding windscreens, the flash of a hothouse, the reek of car-
riage-cloth. At its zenith comes a sweltering crowd of fathers with
seamy foreheads, loud fat mothers and that filthy-minded uncle. In
the last three stanzas Larkin ups the tempo: evening is implicit in the
long shadows of the poplars, a bowler running up is suspended in
the luminescence like the lover who doesn't kiss in 'Ode on a Grecian
Urn'. But it is of another ode – 'To Autumn' – that one thinks. There
is the same arrested lushness of fruition, the same sense of time
hanging in the balance and bringing not decay but fulfilment.

True, you may say, but what about 'The Old Fools', 'The Building', 'Aubade'? Here I can only echo Philip Hobsbaum in perhaps the
most perceptive essay ever written on Larkin, 'Larkin's Singing Line':
'The consolation is in the language'. In Larkin's own words, 'The Old
Fools' is a poem of ambivalent anger. It is in part his rage against the
dying of the light. But in the third stanza a miracle occurs. The rage
is replaced by pity and wonder:

> Each looms
> Like a deep loss restored.

'Restored' combines contradictory meanings. The loss is restored
– the wound is opened afresh – but also restored: the Wordswor-
thian meaning of 'repaired'. This ambivalence prepares us for the
visionary radiance of 'the sun's / Faint friendliness on the wall some
lonely / Rain-ceased midsummer evening' where you virtually melt
into a sensuous state of emotion transcending thought: desolate, but
also 'a visible scene on which the sun is shining'.

I return to the confidence of the language. To invert a phrase
from Larkin's favourite Ian Fleming, it is stirred not shaken. For
Larkin, the battlefront isn't the Somme or Auschwitz, Kosovo or
Ethiopia. It is here, now, in every moment – an unflagging contest
between annihilation and creative retrieval. He doesn't narrow his
vision, he enlarges it. From those vast Russian land- and skyscapes
to the funeral of a prostitute, Larkin is instinct with pity and terror.
In the words of his own obsequy on Tennyson, 'We are confounded
by the range, the colour, the self-confidence of it all.' The man denies,
the poetry affirms.

> Now more than ever seems it rich to die,
> To cease upon the midnight with no pain,
> While thou art pouring forth thy soul abroad
> In such an ecstasy!
>
> John Keats, 'Ode to a Nightingale'

subscribe

Make sure of your copy of *The Reader*
and enjoy big savings *
by taking out a **subscription**:

UK
p&p free

1 year	4 issues	**£24.00**
2 years	8 issues	**£38.00**
3 years	12 issues	**£57.00**

Abroad **
including p&p

1 year	4 issues	**£36.00**
2 years	8 issues	**£57.00**
3 years	12 issues	**£86.00**

Please make cheques payable to the
University of Liverpool and post to
**The Reader, 19 Abercromby Square,
University of Liverpool, L69 7ZG**.

Include your name and address and specify the
issue with which you would like your subscription to begin.

* Save 20% on 2- and 3-year subscriptions
** The easiest way to take out a subscription abroad is by using Paypal
on our website: www.thereader.co.uk

The Reader Crossword

Cassandra   No.15

Across

9. Experiencing lack of will brings about this condition (9)
10. Lulu, for example, turns up in hope rather than real anticipation (5)
11. Inhabitant of China also found in Pennsylvania (5)
*12, 13 down and 28. Circling yard, lions run to reach him (3, 6, 5, 5)
13. All is revealed once lad breaks the porcelain (7)
*14. See 3 down
17. Passages recalled during those moments when we smell a sandalwood tree (5)
19. Litigious lady? (3)
20. Were these Cleopatra's best days for sticking to diet? (5)
21. Candidate has name in French and in Early English (7)
22. She's good at concealing grouse (7)
*24. The sound of sudden heavy rains where our hero allegedly perished (9)
26. Gene's just a day away from Oklahoma city (5)
*28. See 12 across
29. Time can see no change in these people and their language (9)

* Clues with an asterisk have a common theme

Down

1. Fellow important enough but inwardly weak (4)
2. Start of any tune on nose-flute and lyre will produce this music (6)
*3 and 14 across. The story of a smear campaign in Polixenes' kingdom (1, 7, 2, 7)
*4. Medical partner heard to make an enquiry about TV listings (6)
5. Easter 1916 saw the birth of this beauty (8)
*6. How many does this sign denote? (4)
7. House of Lords became hiding place for Louis XIV's saucy steward (8)
8. Market's not bad (4)
*13. See 12 across
*15. Paying respects with final musical performance? (3, 4, 3)
16. Mathematical reptile (5)
18. We may save our souls at random by these means (8)
*19 and 23. Our hero finds shell shock more upsetting (8, 6)
22. Washing down hogs in mess (6)
*23. See 19 down
24. Inside, a picture of grandad adorns the bottom half of the wall (4)
25. No charge to deliver (4)
27. Final word usually in agreement (4)

Horses for Courses

1. Which rider caused the racehorse Frou Frou to fall, 'her neck fluttering on the ground at his feet like a wounded bird'?

2. In *The Faerie Queene*, which horse is distinguished by a black spot on its mouth like a horseshoe?

3. 'I heard a sudden harmony of hooves, / And, turning, saw afar / A hundred snowy horses unconfined.' Where were these horses seen?

4. In which novel do John Grady Cole and Lacey Rawlins saddle up their horses and ride south?

5. Which horse was killed when the pointed shaft of the morning mikcart entered his breast 'like a sword'?

6. Where did Boxer and Clover live?

7. 'And I saw my stout galloper Roland at last, / With resolute shoulders, each butting away / The haze, as some bluff river headland its spray.' Where was Roland galloping towards?

8. Who did Rosinante belong to?

9. 'The horses started and for the last time / I watched the clods crumble and topple over / After the ploughshare and the stumbling team.' What is the unusual title of this poem?

10. Who created the mythical 'Black Bess'?

11. In which novel do lost souls seek purpose in the Depression by taking part in a dance marathon?

12. Who dreams of a drunken peasant ferociously beating his horse and the crowd of spectators joining in, for fun?

13. Which racehorse killed his trainer, John Straker?

14. 'In a sort of lightning of knowledge their movement travelled through her, the quiver and strain and thrust of their powerful flanks, as they burst before her and drew on, beyond.' Who encounters these horses?

15. Who described his horse as coming from 'the earliest time of the world. No man had ever ridden him before. By day his coat was like silver, by night like unseen shade'?

16. According to Shakespeare, who did 'White Surrey' belong to?

17. 'I saw the horses. / Huge in the dense grey – ten together – / Megalith still.' Which poet had this vision?

18. Diamond 'had without the slightest warning exhibited…a most vicious energy in kicking and just missed killing the groom.' Which young man's hopes were dashed with Diamond's misfortune?

19. Which short story was published in a collection put together by Lady Cynthia Asquith, a friend of the author's? Critics have argued that the characters are modelled on Asquith and her autistic son.

20. Not exactly literary, but The Buck can't resist…What are the names of the horses belonging to The Lone Ranger and Tonto?

Contributors 23

Adrian Blackledge has published poems in a wide range of journals. A former winner of the Eric Gregory Award, his first volume, *Green Eyes*, was published in 2005 by Pikestaff Press.

Keith Edwin Colwell was born in Liverpool and lives in Wirral. He once taught in Adult and Continuing Education and is trying to get his first novel published while working on a second.

Wendy Cook was born a Bury Black Pudding and now lives in Helmshore (where she educates people small and tall) and Cumbria (where she gardens, stitches, reads, writes and rambles).

Denise Cottrell Boyce read Theology at Keble College, Oxford. Since then she has selflessly dedicated her life to raising her seven children, asking nothing in return but their undying devotion and unswerving obedience.

Neil Curry's study of the eighteenth-century poet Christopher Smart was published in 2005. His most recent collection of poems is *The Road to Gunpowder House* (Enitharmon Press).

Philip Davis is a professor of English at the University of Liverpool. He has published *The Victorians* (OUP, 2002), edited a collection of religious verse, *All the Days of My Life* (Dent, 1999), and is currently writing a biography of Bernard Malamud.

Terence Davies was born in Liverpool in 1945. His films include *Distant Voices, Still Lives* (1988), *The Long Day Closes* (1992) and his adaptation of *The House of Mirth* (2000).

Susan Duncan is a consultant neurologist at the Neurosciences Centre in Greater Manchester. She has a special interest in epilepsy.

Jean Edmunds was born in 1935, Brightlingsea, Essex, and has spent most of her life in South Africa, returning to England for good in 2004. Her short stories, poetry and articles have had some success in South Africa and the UK.

Susan Fox's poems have appeared in many journals including *Poetry*, *Boulevard* and *The Paris Review*. An opera to her libretto about a hidden child during WWII had its semi-professional premiere in New York. She lives in the French countryside.

Harriet Gordon Getzels was once an American ex-pat living in Britain but is now a British ex-pat living in America. She is a filmmaker and writer on a perennial search for identity; but not her own.

Marleen Hacquoil moved from Canada to her husband's native island several years ago and joined the Monday Group shortly thereafter, replacing hectic city life with the stimulating company of keen readers.

Jen Hadfield is a poet and photographer whose first collection, Almanacs, was published by Bloodaxe this year. Her website is http://www.rogue-seeds.co.uk

Suzanne Hodge is a research associate in the Health and Community Care Research Unit at the University of Liverpool. Her research interests cluster round the theme of communication in healthcare.

Ann Jay is a general practitioner who has been listening to patients' stories for 25 years. She has an MA in Medical Humanities and lives in West Wales.

Karen King-Aribisala is professor of English at the University of Lagos.

Her book *Our Wife and Other Stories* won the Best First Book Prize (African Region) Commonwealth Literature (1990–91). Her novel *Kicking Tongues* was published by Heinemann (1998–99).

Mark Leech's book of translations, *Anglo-Saxon Voices*, is published by Pipers' Ash Ltd. He won the Stephen Spender poetry translation prize in 2004. He lives in Oxford.

Richard Livermore's work has appeared in numerous magazines and also in book form. He edits *Chanticleer Magazine* and is presently preparing a volume of essays, with an introduction by Jeremy Reed.

Patrick McGuinness is Reader in French and Comparative Literature at the University of Oxford and a fellow of St Anne's College. His first book of poems, *The Canals of Mars* (Carcanet) has just appeared in Italian as *I Canali di Marte*. His translation of Mallarmé's *For Anatole's Tomb* was a PBS recommendation.

Robin Philipp is a New Zealander and graduate of the University of Otago. He is a Consultant Occupational and Public Health Physician in the Bristol Royal Infirmary, England.

Anna Pollard studied English as a mature student at Manchester Metropolitan University. Since graduating in 1997 she has worked as a freelance proofreader. She is currently writing a collection of poetry about living with epilepsy.

John Redmond teaches Creative Writing at the University of Liverpool. He has written a poetry collection, *Thumb's Width* (Carcanet, 2001) and a textbook, *How to Write a Poem* (Blackwell, 2005).

Thelma Rondel is Jersey-born and Jersey-bred and all her life she has been an avid reader. The Monday Group has stimulated interest since 1981.

Ann Stapleton is a freelance writer from Ohio whose work has appeared or is forthcoming in *The Dark Horse*, *Alaska Quarterly Review*, and *The Weekly Standard*.

Pauline Suett-Barbieri was born in Liverpool. She was shortlisted for the Exeter and Bridport Prizes and has a collection with Waterloo Press (2006). An ancestor, Richard Suett, the Shakespearean clown, was a favourite of George III and Charles Lamb.

Enid Stubin is Assistant Professor of English at Kingsborough Community College of the City University of New York and Adjunct Professor of Humanities at New York University's School of Continuing and Professional Studies.

Michele A. Sweeten lives in Austin, Texas, where she works as an accountant and schools her three children at home. She is a novice author.

Ray Tallis is now a full-time writer after 30 years as a doctor. His trilogy on human consciousness, *Handkind*, was published 2003–5. He has just finished *Unthinkable Thought: The Enduring Significance of Parmenides*.

Laura Webb is from Merseyside. She worked and studied in Spain for a year before attending Manchester University, where she is currently an English undergraduate.

Mary Weston was born in Hawaii and now lives in Liverpool. She is a facilitator for the community-based project Get Into Reading. Her novel *The Escape Plan* was published in 2001.

Stephen Wilson is the author of *The Cradle of Violence: Essays on Psychiatry, Psychoanalysis and Literature* (Jessica Kingsley, 1995). He has had poems in the *LRB*, *New Welsh Review*, *Rialto* and other magazines.

Buck's Quiz 21

1. John Milton, 'Lycidas' 2. P. B. Shelley, 'To a Skylark' 3. Christopher Marlowe, *Edward II* 4. John Keats, 'Ode to a Nightingale 5. Thomas Gray, 'Elegy Written in a Country Churchyard' 6. John Webster, *The White Devil* 7. Alexander Pope, *An Essay on Criticism* 8. Julia Ward Howe, 'Battle Hymn of the Republic' 9. John Donne, *Devotions upon Emergent Occasions* 10. Rupert Brooke, 'The Old Vicarage, Grantchester' 11. Ernest Dowson, 'Non Sum Qualis Eram' 12. John Milton, *Paradise Lost* 13. William Shakespeare, *The Tempest* 14. A. E. Housman, *A Shropshire Lad* 15. Virgil, *The Aeneid* 16. William Shakespeare, *Julius Caesar* 17. The Koran 18. The Bible and Robert Burns 'To A Mouse' 19. John Milton, *Paradise Lost* 20. Xenophon

Please send your answers to Buck's Quiz, The Reader, 19 Abercromby Square, Liverpool L69 7ZG

Cassandra Crossword 14

Across

9. Hierarchy 10. Abash 11. Tuesday 12. Far from 13. Unit 14. Dislocated 16. Pesetas 17. Biriani 19. Thoughtful 22. Smug 24. Agitato 25. Emperor 26. Okapi 27. An eyebrow

Down

1. The Trumpet Major 2. Remedies 3. Hardy 4. Acrylics 5. Eyeful 6. Capricorn 7. Parrot 8. The Madding Crowd 15. Stigmatic 17. Blue Eyes 18. Admirers 20. Ogival 21. Thomas 23. Ypres

Distribution Information

For trade orders in all territories except North America and Mexico, please contact:
Marston Book Services, PO Box 269, Abingdon, OX14 4YN, UK
Tel: +44 [0]1235 465 500   **Fax:** +44 [0]1235 465 555
Email: trade.order@marston.co.uk   **Web:** www.marston.co.uk

For trade orders in North America and Mexico, please contact:
University of Chicago Press, 1427 East 60th Street, Chicago, Illinois 60637, USA
Tel: +1 800 621 2736   **Fax:** +1 800 621 8476
Email: custserv@press.uchicago.edu   **Web:** www.press.uchicago.edu

For institutional subscriptions in all territories, please contact:
Sarah Preece, Subscriptions, Marston Book Services Ltd, PO Box 269, Abingdon, Oxfordshire, OX14 4YN, UK
Tel: +44 [0]1235 465 537   **Email:** subscriptions@marston.co.uk

If you have any queries regarding trade orders or institutional subscriptions, please contact Janet Smith at Liverpool University Press on +44 [0]151 794 2233 or email janmar@liv.ac.uk